THIS MAN'S ARMY

THIS MAN'S ARMY

A Soldier's Story From the Front Lines
of the War on Terrorism

Andrew Exum

GOTHAM BOOKS

GOTHAM BOOKS
Published by Penguin Group (USA) Inc.
375 Hudson Street, New York, New York 10014, U.S.A.
Penguin Books Ltd, Registered Offices: 80 Strand, London WC2R 0RL, England
Penguin Books Australia Ltd, 250 Camberwell Road,
Camberwell, Victoria 3124, Australia
Penguin Books Canada Ltd, 10 Alcorn Avenue,
Toronto, Ontario, Canada M4V 3B2
Penguin Books (NZ) Ltd, Cnr Rosedale and Airborne Roads,
Albany, Auckland 1310, New Zealand

Published by Gotham Books, a division of Penguin Group (USA) Inc.

First printing, June 2004
1   3   5   7   9   10   8   6   4   2

Gotham Books and the skyscraper logo are trademarks of Penguin Group (USA) Inc.

ISBN: 1-592-40063-9

Printed in the United States of America
Set in Bulmer MT with Arepo Bold
Designed by Sabrina Bowers

This book is printed on acid-free paper. ∞

THIS BOOK IS DEDICATED TO THE MEN OF THIRD PLATOON,
A COMPANY, 4TH BATTALION, 31ST INFANTRY, 2001–2002

We would not die in that man's company
That fears his fellowship to die with us.
—SHAKESPEARE, *Henry V*

Danger gleams like sunshine to a brave man's eyes.
—EURIPIDES

PROLOGUE

MARCH 2002

BAGRAM AIRBASE, AFGHANISTAN

THE SUN ROSE over the mountains to the east, flooding the
valley with light. While it remained dark, we could still tease
ourselves into thinking that the job we had to do today was
some way off. But the sun, creeping up over the Hindu Kush,
reminded us of the immediacy of our fate. We knew that the
time had arrived for us to be brave, so that we might continue
to believe that we were, even if we should face the worst.

We quickly formed up in the new sunlight, walking in a
line toward the waiting helicopters. We moved with great labor, each of us carrying nearly his body weight in weapons
and equipment.

It was an ungodly amount of gear. I personally carried
ninety pounds of equipment in my rucksack as well as 210
rounds of ammunition, a radio, a set of maps, a compass, a
handheld global positioning system, and two quarts of water.

I had an array of other assorted supplies strapped to the nylon webbing on my body armor, including four grenades with phrases like "Duck!" and "You Should Have Dodged Left!" scribbled on them in black Magic Marker. I wondered how well I was going to move at ten thousand feet above sea level with all this crap on my body. We helped one another down off our feet in order to sit on the tarmac while waiting for our CH-47 helicopters to fuel. Then we sat silently, watching the planes and attack helicopters take off a few hundred meters away.

Finally, it was our turn to load the helicopters, and each man struggled to his feet under the weight of his equipment. One of my friends from another platoon walked over and shook my hand before he went to board his own helicopter. He didn't say anything, just squeezed my gloved hand in his and forced a tight-lipped smile. Another friend in his group threw me a cocky wink, too far away already to walk over.

It took a while to load the bird. We packed in tight, and because I would be one of the first on the ground, I was one of the last to board. Few of us had awakened early enough to eat anything in the hours before sunrise, and those of us who did had not been able to eat much. After we settled into the helicopter, a few men tugged at their pockets for energy bars or granola they had stowed away in their shirts and camouflage cargo pants. Most looked around nervously, their helmets swiveling from left to right. The curved night vision mounts strapped to their foreheads made them look like rhinos from the neck up.

I almost fell over when the helicopter took off. There were more than thirty of us inside, and like me, many were on the floor, sitting on their rucksacks. The body armor wrapped around my torso made me feel awkward and off-balance, and when the helicopter lifted off, I latched onto Flash, my radio operator, to steady myself. Once the helicopter was in the air and on its way, we righted ourselves and settled down for the ride into combat.

The helicopter had machine gunners on both sides, as well as one on the back ramp, which was down. The gunner in the back sat on the very edge of the ramp, confident he would not fall because he was tied down to the helicopter by a four-foot tether. We got our first good aerial view of the base as we left. Below us, rows of tan tents shuddered under the rotor wash of the helicopter blades. Behind them, we could see the bombed-out airplane hangar that had become the division's headquarters.

I looked around me at the men to my right and left. They were *my* men, and I could feel them looking at me as well. Some of them looked scared, others simply looked anxious, and still others feigned sleep in an effort to show how cool they could be, how detached they were about what we were about to do. Many were still just kids, no more than eighteen years old, yet they carried a dizzying array of machine guns, shotguns, explosives, and other weapons. Only one man in the platoon, my platoon sergeant, was much older than thirty, and he was sitting near me by the ramp, next to the mortar rounds we had loaded onto an ATV that was lashed to the floor of the helicopter.

The helicopter gathered speed, cruising over the hills and through the valleys of eastern Afghanistan. The only good view was out the back, but it was spectacular. A few minutes after we left the base, we began to ascend and crested a ridge, only to swoop down the other side, flying low and close to the ground. It made for a heck of a ride. We soon leveled out, and I could see power lines stretching from east to west. I knew we must be near Kabul, the capital city. No other place in the country had any power lines, much less any other utility.

We made our way south of the capital and then headed due southeast toward Gardez and into the valley to that city's east, the Shah-e-Kot Valley, where American and allied forces had been fighting with Taliban and al-Qaeda forces for the past week. As we got closer, the terrain grew more mountainous. The ride got rockier too, as the pilots protected their helicopters from snipers and rockets by hugging the ground, flying what they called "map of the earth."

We had been in the air for over an hour when one of my soldiers, Noodles, unceremoniously puked his meager breakfast up into a plastic bag between his legs. (He had been given his name by the platoon for the way his thin arms shook like wet noodles when he tried to do push-ups.) The other soldiers in the helicopter roared in approval, shouting and cheering Noodles on as he vomited. The crew chief had just enough time to throw the bag out the back of the helicopter before another soldier, Tayo, also puked, losing it into a Ziploc bag that had just a few seconds earlier contained one of my team leaders' cans of Copenhagen. Once again, the other soldiers cheered Tayo, wildly yelling and egging him on. It reminded me of the times I had been about to jump out of an airplane and seen motion sickness spread through the plane, with guys puking into the little yellow bags the air force hands out prior to takeoff.

I knew that today it was more than motion sickness. Despite the hooting and hollering, the embarrassed grin on Noodles's face, and Tayo's brave shouts back to his platoon mates, I saw the raw fear behind the smiles. Fear was behind the yelling too, a welcome release for the other soldiers in the helicopter, who now had something to take their minds off the fact that we were about to be dropped into the middle of a suspected al-Qaeda stronghold and that some of us might not make it back to the place we had just left.

I was scared too. I had lived with and led these men for more than a year. We had become a family, and they were my brothers. White, black, Hispanic, Asian—we looked like the United Colors of Benetton and yet were as close as any group of men can be, more so than any athletic team I ever played on and more so than even the friends I had grown up with back home in Tennessee. I knew everything about the guys around me—their hometowns, the names of their brothers and sisters and girlfriends, their favorite bands, what their parents did for a living, how old they were when they lost their virginity, the color of their first car. Everything—even the stuff I had no interest in knowing.

I was pretty damn sure I had the stomach to kill or be killed, but I wasn't sure if I could watch anyone else in this helicopter die. I looked at my platoon sergeant. Sergeant Montoya looked back at me, eye-to-eye, and we instantly knew we were thinking the same thing. The soldiers in the platoon called him Yoda behind his back because he knew everything and had lived to the incredibly advanced age of thirty-four. He had prayed over me the night before, asking God to give me the judgment and skill necessary to bring the platoon back safely. We were both professional soldiers, but the men under our care were more than Department of Defense cannon fodder to be indiscriminately thrown to their deaths. We cared for these men more than we cared for ourselves, and we were resolved to bring them all back alive.

I broke away from Sergeant Montoya's gaze and began to tie a piece of string to my right wrist. It had become a combat ritual for me, beginning with the first mission we had run a few days earlier. Before we landed, I tied a piece of parachute cord to my wrist. At home today, I have a collection of string bracelets I fashioned before missions, and there are enough to cover much of my forearm.

I closed my eyes to pray. I told God I was about to take leave of my faith for a few days. When I opened my eyes, I would be a new person, a person outside myself.

A while later, my radioman, Flash, reached back and tapped me on the shoulder.

"Sir," he said. "We're close."

I struggled to reach my feet and leaned over Junk, one of my machine gunners, to get a view out of one of the Chinook's tiny side windows. I saw small dark figures on the ridge to the helicopter's left and knew these were our allies, Canadian soldiers who had landed before us and were securing the landing zone. I then helped Flash to his feet and worked hard to remain upright as I put my rucksack on and then secured Flash's radio to his back.

As the Chinook settled down, the dust flew up, obscuring everything and blinding us all. We felt a sharp jolt, and Flash and I grabbed onto each other again to keep from falling over.

The back ramp filled with dust, and the machine gunner on the ramp moved to the side.

We couldn't see a thing, but it was time. I pushed the men ahead of me, pulling Flash with my left hand, and before I knew it, I was out of the helicopter, under its spinning blades.

I had just set foot into the Shah-e-Kot Valley.

I

I GREW UP in East Tennessee, just outside the medium-sized city of Chattanooga. If ever there was a Southern city rooted in the past and struggling to find its path in modern America, Chattanooga was it. I was born half a mile from Missionary Ridge, site of one of the bloodiest battles of the Civil War. Cannons stand on all the high points of the city, guarding historical markers, standing sentinel for an era that died at the Appomattox Courthouse over a century before I was born. At least postbellum Chattanooga was more forward thinking than some of the cities even farther south. It had a thriving urban renewal program and could boast that most of its inhabitants heartily enjoyed living there.

I certainly did. I spent my adolescence playing football, running track, and doing all the normal things boys my age did. I was always small, until I hit puberty, late, in my junior year of high school, but I loved the outdoors and felt comfortable there in a way I never did on the athletic fields. I loved the mountains and sandstone cliffs that surrounded my home, and hiking and running along the dirt paths that led through the woods. In addition to being an agile rock climber, I was an avid reader. So when the sun was shining, I climbed. When it rained, I stayed inside and read. It was a simple childhood, and I felt blessed.

My father was a journalist and newspaper executive, my mother an English teacher at a girls' school in Chattanooga. They were divorced when I was eight, and after that I lived with my mom and younger sister, learning to be somewhat independent at an early age. My mother would leave for work with my sister in the early hours of the morning and return late at night. To earn extra money for my sister and me to have what we needed, she worked as an assistant to her school's basketball coach in the afternoons and evenings. I rarely saw her during the school week. I got myself up every morning and fixed most of my meals myself or ate them at school.

I was lucky to be able to attend a distinguished Southern boys' boarding school on partial scholarship as a day student, the result of my mother's work as a teacher at the crosstown girls' school. My father paid generous child support to my mother and contributed the rest of my high school tuition but, significantly, didn't plan on college. Or, I should say, he didn't plan on my going to college where I did.

He's a good guy, my father, but he had been a notorious hell-raiser when he was a teen. He went through six different high schools before finally graduating on a cold day in December. They sent him his diploma in the mail.

He went on to the University of Mississippi, where he partied hard and paid his way through his first semester by selling beer to all the fraternities and sororities on the black market. Oxford, Mississippi, was a dry town then, and my father used to drive a tractor-trailer full of kegs from West Memphis, Arkansas, making a tidy profit when he returned to school. This story was confirmed to me by some of my friends' parents who went to Ole Miss with my father, so unlike some of the more apocryphal stories about Dad, I'm inclined to believe it. He left school after a year, his departure no doubt hastened by the fact that he had urinated in the dean's convertible one night while drunk. It didn't matter, though. My father's future was assured, working for his grandfather at the local newspaper.

His own father was a brilliant academic who had long since drank his life away by the time my father left for college, divorcing my grandmother and cutting himself off from his own family. In his final years, the only members of the family he still spoke to were my sister and me. He had reformed himself by that point and used to tell us stories of his early life in Faulkner's Mississippi just down the road from his friend, the novelist and editor Willie Morris. He had moved to Chattanooga just before World War II and married into one of the oldest families in the city, the McDonalds. They had fled Scotland after the infamous Glen Coe massacre of 1692, to Ireland and then to Virginia, eventually moving west to settle on a small plot of land in East Tennessee in 1819. We have held the same piece of land ever since.

My father raised me to shoot rifles. He could never throw a football or baseball with me on account of his bum right arm that had been crushed when he flipped a Jeep onto it in 1973. So instead of playing sports, he would take me to our family farm and teach me how to shoot with a single-shot Winchester. He sat with me for hours while I fired at paper targets and cans sitting on the fence. When I was twelve, I got a .22-caliber rifle of my own. My father taught me how to control my breathing while taking aim, how to hold the rifle's butt tight into my shoulder, and how to gently squeeze the trigger instead of jerking it with my finger. We would sit high on a hill above a small stream, where my father would smoke cigars and drink Diet Cokes while I shot at targets he chose. Often, he would give me his empty Coke cans and make me run down the hill, put them in the stream, sprint back up the hill, grab my rifle, steady my heavy breathing, and fire enough holes into the cans to sink them before they could float away out of range. Eventually, he let me roam the woods of our farm alone to hunt snakes with the big farm dogs we kept around.

IF MY FATHER'S family held a genteel aura of Southern aristocracy, my mother's family was firmly rooted in the lower middle classes. Her father grew up on a small tobacco farm in South Carolina, moving to Chattanooga to begin a career as a photographer after serving in the Pacific during the Second World War. Her mother was from Louisiana, a former high school basketball star in the days of six-on-six half-court girls' basketball, who met my grandfather while working in New Orleans. He had a son from a previous marriage, and with my grandmother had three daughters. My mother was the second and would graduate from the University of Tennessee along with her sisters.

No one I have spoken to can understand why my mother and father ever married. My father's family and friends always figured he would marry someone from a more distinguished family, and my mother's family wondered how my mother—responsible, educated, down-to-earth—could fall in love with someone so obviously different from her. My father was charming but as wild and irresponsible as my mother was calm and balanced. I guess my mother saw in my father someone fun and unpredictable, as well as a young man with considerable talents. Writing a popular sports column for the newspaper, about the only thing that everyone in East Tennessee cares about, football, my father wrote with an understanding of his readers unmatched by any other writer I have ever read. He wrote for the common man reading the afternoon paper after a long day at work, and it was impossible to go places with my father and not be accosted by a fan of his column. In my mother, my father saw someone who could raise his children to be more responsible than he was.

After my parents divorced, my mother went along raising my sister and me just as my father had wanted, in her image—responsible, full of common sense, shunning anything flashy or ostentatious. Both my parents are of Scottish descent, but I got my Scotch frugality—short arms and long pockets, you might say—from my mother. My father was and is a legendary spender, always in debt. But I have inherited as many traits from my father as my mother. He was always hardworking, which impressed my mother when she met him, often holding down multiple jobs and reporting to work at the paper our family owned as early as four in the morning. When the workers at our paper went on strike in the seventies, my father worked twenty-hour days alongside the rest of the family, writing stories, operating the presses, and catching naps on the sofa. The strike broke after a few weeks, a defeat for the labor movement in the South but a proud moment for the family.

During high school, I took hard courses, studied equally hard, and took pride in my work. I also participated in a lot of extracurricular activities, relishing the leadership opportunities sports and student government provided. Playing varsity football during my sophomore year, I was not only the smallest player on the team but the smallest in all of Tennessee. I played free safety weighing only 105 pounds but discovered that toughness often gets you farther than size and athleticism. All the same, I was knocked unconscious two times that season trying to tackle fullbacks twice my size.

My father was supportive when it came to football, always in the stands, and only criticized me once, during my senior season. Before one of our away games, I walked to the middle of the field to shake hands with the other team's captains and call the coin toss. Afterward, I ran back to the sideline and played a tough game, which we lost, barely, to the team that would eventually go on to win the state championship. After the game, my father was waiting for me on the way to the team bus, a stern look on his face. Before he'd allow me to board the bus, he let me know in no uncertain terms that he had seen me shake hands with the other team's captains before the game and fail to take off my thin leather receiving gloves beforehand, which he considered an unforgivable breach of courtesy.

"Just who the hell do you think you play for," he asked me, "the University of Miami?"

For my father, winning or losing wasn't as important as playing with class.

Academically, I did well and only performed poorly in one subject—Latin, during my freshman year. But I would redeem myself in the classics three years later by becoming a National Greek Scholar as a senior. My college counselor steered me toward challenging, competitive schools. While my father had always assumed I would go to the University of Tennessee (like my mother) or someplace equally cheap, I instead set off with my mother in her Saturn station wagon the summer before my senior year, to look at the elite—and expensive—schools of the Northeast before summer football practice began. After eighteen years in Chattanooga, I was becoming restless for a change of scenery.

My father, I think, would have been somewhat happy if I had chosen the University of Virginia—a proper school for a good Southern gentleman to attend. But when I visited there, they told me they could care less whether I applied there or not. "We already get the best applicants from all over the South," they assured me.

That turned me off, and I decided on the University of Pennsylvania before my senior year began. I liked the urban environment at Penn, the big libraries, and the diversity of the student body. I had never before seen such a multicolored group of people, speaking so many languages. I liked the energy of the city and of the campus. The Penn admissions officer who visited my high school took a liking to me and made me her personal mission to recruit. I applied early and got in shortly after football season ended.

I now had a bigger problem, which was how to pay for a school that would cost $30,000 a year. When I came to my father and pled my case for tuition, all I got was shrugged shoulders. My mother and I applied for financial aid, but my father's considerable income counted against us—he made a good bit but had saved nothing for my college and had heavy debt. At the time I was really angry at Dad's remarkable dual absence, of both foresight and fiscal responsibility, but as I got older and came to learn the full extent of my father's debt, my anger turned to pity. He's the only one in our tightfisted family who isn't by nature a cheapskate, and the hole he's dug for himself over the years inspires silent frustration more than rage. It was difficult back then for me to see how a man who wrote so effortlessly, so beautifully, could be so incompetent in other areas of his life. But it was hard to stay angry with the old man, and if you know my father you understand. Eventually his ebullient, charismatic, larger-than-life personality just wears you down, until you forget why you were angry with him in the first place.

So I quit running track and began working at the family newspaper after school in addition to the weekends I already worked. By the end of the year, I had saved $10,000 from three years of working during high school and my mother came up with another $8,000—enough for a year of Penn when combined with the financial aid I received. However, it was understood that to stay at Penn beyond my freshman year I would have to get some additional help.

The military immediately became an option. I had always

wanted to serve my country and had toyed with the idea of enlisting for two years before college. But my college counselor, coaches, and teachers recommended that I try for an ROTC scholarship instead.

I felt that as long as I was going to join the military, I was going to go all the way. I had always loved the woods and any sort of physical challenge, and I didn't want to be some desk jockey or supply lackey wearing a uniform. I wanted to be a killer. I wanted to be something elite, like a Navy SEAL or Army Ranger. I wanted to be something I could brag about when I got old.

The Army presented the best options, so when I visited Penn again after I had been accepted, I also visited the Army ROTC program there. They were excited to see me and signed me up right away, with the assurance that I could apply for a three-year scholarship once I started school.

I spent that summer climbing, growing my hair long, and working for my dad at the newspaper. It was the summer of the Atlanta Olympics, and I would drive the hour and a half to Atlanta every day to get enough interviews with athletes to supply me with a few days' worth of stories for the sports section. I was usually off work in time to climb some routes on the sandstone cliffs behind my house before the sun set. I loved the way the rock felt under my fingers, the way that my forearms burned from hanging for so long, the way that adrenaline alone often kept me from falling. The backs of my hands were always cut or covered with scabs from having jammed my fists into cracks as I pulled myself up the cliffs.

In September, my mother and I packed her station wagon and drove north, up I-81 through Virginia to Washington, D.C., and then up I-95 into Philadelphia. We started the day in the green lushness of East Tennessee and ended it on I-76, driving through the oil refinery and housing projects of west Philadelphia. I was beginning to see what Walker Percy, one of my favorite writers, meant in his novel *The Moviegoer* when he described the "rinsing, wrenching sadness of the cities of the North."

My freshman year of college was a disaster. I was lost in the city, lost in my classes, and felt isolated as a white Southern kid among all those Yankees. My accent, which I had never considered pronounced, evidently *was*, and it just made things worse. Each time I spoke up in class, I could feel my classmates thinking I must be either ignorant, inbred, or racist. Maybe even all three. I didn't think I belonged and wanted to go home. I even considered transferring to the University of Virginia. My Northern classmates all seemed so much smarter than me. In the novel *White Noise* by Don DeLillo, one of the characters responds that he knows so much because, of course, "I'm from New York." Many of my classmates were the same way, believing themselves to be street smart and wise beyond their years. I understand now that they were just as scared and unsure of themselves as I was, but I didn't know it then. While my classmates worked hard in the library and achieved good grades, I began to take my failures in the classroom to be a matter of course and adopted a defeatist attitude.

The Army was different from the rest of Penn. I was good at ROTC from the start. I knew how to navigate in the woods better than the Northerners, even in the flat woods of New Jersey, where we trained on weekends. I could outshoot any of them with an M-16, and I made easy friends. They jokingly called me "Sergeant York" after Tennessee's famous war hero, a moniker that pleased me to no end. I liked waking up early on Wednesday morning to drill, and learned how to perform exotic tasks like clearing bunkers and hallways with guns and grenades. I liked wearing a uniform, which made me look different from the rest of my classmates for at least one day during the week. On Mondays, I would report to military science class to learn about the rank structure and how the army organized itself. We also took classes in basic military tactics and leadership. I never made anything less than an A in ROTC, but unfortunately, I wasn't making *A*'s in anything else. Despite my poor grades, the Army gave me a scholarship that summer. My mother gave me a big hug when she heard the news. We didn't tell my father until a few days later, but when he heard he greeted the news with a mixture of pride and apprehension. He was proud I had decided to serve in the military, but I don't think he'd planned on me showing so much resolve to stay up north for college.

Sophomore year wasn't any easier, though. My grades in the fall were the worst yet. In the spring, a particularly ugly (and absurd) classroom incident reminded me of how much of an outsider I still was. After becoming angry with me while arguing in class about whether or not order was restored at the end of Shakespeare's *Measure for Measure*, one girl called me "David Duke" in retort to my argument. I guess she figured associating me with the modern South's most famous racist would shut me up and prove her intellectual superiority, but given the argument's context, the insult was a non sequitur. It was just an ugly slur from a Yankee prep school girl suddenly alarmed that she was being bested in argument by a backward Southerner.

I got mad and walked out of class. I returned the next week only after a black girl who usually sat by me in the class tracked me down and let me know how embarrassed the rest of the class was for what that girl had said.

ROTC wasn't as fun that year, either. In part because of recent protests that surrounded the ROTC presence on campus, the Army decided to merge the Penn Army ROTC program with all the other programs in the city. We now met at the Drexel Armory, which was only a few blocks from campus, but we were no longer a tangible part of the Penn community as we had been a year earlier.

I was angry about the protests. During the Vietnam conflict, college students protested ROTC as a way to protest the war in Southeast Asia. Now a small but committed group of activists on campus protested ROTC to complain about how the "Don't Ask, Don't Tell" policy established by President Clinton and Congress discriminated against homosexuals. For my part, all I wanted to do was serve my country and pay for school, and it pissed me off that ROTC was moved off campus to placate a noisy special interest group that had a beef with a policy set up not by the army but by elected officials in Washington. To the protesters' credit, they never directly confronted the cadets. My gay friends openly appreciated that I was just trying to pay for college, but that didn't stop them from sometimes lashing out at me.

That summer, I took off immediately after passing my Ancient Greece exam at the beginning of May, so that I could begin training with the military at the U.S. Army Airborne School in Fort Benning, Georgia, a week later. Airborne School was my first real experience in the regular army, away from ROTC, and I passed with flying colors. For the first two weeks, we trained in sawdust pits and on towers meant to simulate jumping out of an airplane. In the third week, we jumped out of an airplane five times and graduated at the end of the week. During the course, I lived in the drab army barracks at Fort Benning and tried my best to be as anonymous as possible in training, to avoid the ire of "the black hats," as the Airborne instructors were known. When we were given time off, I sat in the room I shared with another soldier and read the books I had brought with me. I remember a Navy SEAL who was going through the course with me asking me about the book I was reading one morning, Vladimir Nabokov's *Lolita*. I didn't know how to explain it and mumbled something about the book being a narrative of a road trip between a man and his stepdaughter.

"Sounds pretty fucking boring," he replied.

"It is," I assured him.

I was proud to earn the silver wings identifying me as a paratrooper at the end of the month. Full of confidence, I resolved to turn things around at Penn when I returned for my junior year.

I did. My grades soared that fall, and I found professors who took an interest in mentoring me. One, a fellow East Tennessee native, even took me aside and let me know that any kid from East Tennessee *couldn't* do worse than an A in his class. The act of fraternal motivation worked. I responded by working my ass off for him as a token of gratitude and as a protest on behalf of all Southerners trapped in Philadelphia.

During his office hours on Wednesdays, I would go in to talk with him, more about football and the University of Tennessee's opponent that upcoming Saturday than anything relating to class. The Tennessee Volunteers were unbeatable that season, going undefeated on their way toward winning the national championship, and I mirrored their success in academic halls above the Mason-Dixon Line.

I earned a varsity letter that fall playing lightweight football, a peculiar sport found only in the Ivy League and at the service academies. It's contact football played only by those weighing less than 165 pounds. A wide receiver and defensive back in high school, I now played defensive end. I enjoyed putting the pads back on again and, despite two broken bones in my left hand, played well enough that season to help us win the league championship. Our only loss that year was to West Point, who was always the dirtiest team we played against.

I also began to assert myself as a campus leader that year. I wrote a column each week for the school newspaper, served as president of my fraternity, and at the end of the year was selected for membership in one of the two exclusive senior honor societies.

ROTC picked up its intensity as well. During sophomore year, most of the classes we were taught had been the same as those we took as freshmen. Now, as juniors, we taught most of the Wednesday morning classes ourselves and were evaluated by the seniors. The ROTC battalion was divided up into four companies, and all the Penn cadets were in one company. I was the company first sergeant, responsible for ensuring that everyone was present for training, had their hair trimmed

every week, and remembered to iron their uniforms and pol-
ish their boots. Keeping track of so many college students,
who during the week all did their own separate thing aside
from ROTC, was like herding cats, but we had fun. Every
other week, I got the Penn cadets together to drink beer and
complain about school and ROTC.

That summer, I went to ROTC Advanced Camp at Fort
Lewis, Washington, for five weeks of leadership training with
upcoming seniors from other colleges across the country. We
all had to meet a group of standards, but they were ridiculously easy, especially the physical requirements. All the activities catered to the lowest common denominator, and the
biggest challenge we faced came in the form of living with female cadets in the same barracks, with only one latrine and
shower room. Every day, we were given an hour to shower after the day's activities, and the eight females insisted they
needed as much time in the latrine as the twenty-two males in
the barracks. The males usually got in the shower last, and by
time we did, the water was almost always cold.

I then more or less "interned" with the 82nd Airborne Division at Fort Bragg for three weeks, jumping out of planes
again and getting a feel for regular army life. I was deeply impressed by the men I worked with there and felt like an im-
poster among them. I felt like the cadet in Tolstoy's *The
Cossacks*, who goes to live and work with the tsar's heartiest
warriors. I did my best to fit in, always volunteering to carry
the heaviest pack, and slowly earning the grudging respect of
the other men. I was quick with a joke and never complained,
so eventually the seasoned sergeants stopped resenting the
fact that in a year I would be making more money than all of

them as an officer, despite having never yet served a day in the active duty military.

Also that summer, my father and I took a trip to France on the occasion of my twenty-first birthday to see the battlefields of Normandy. We walked the length of Omaha Beach one morning and—in the afternoon—visited the American cemetery there. My father began to tear up as soon as we stepped foot onto the pristine, immaculately groomed grounds, and I too was overwhelmed by emotion as I walked by the thousands of tiny white crosses marking the graves of so many brave U.S. servicemen. I had a tough time believing I could ever live up to their example of service and sacrifice.

When I returned to Penn that next fall, I found myself eagerly looking forward to the coming semester for the first time. I had by this time fallen in love with Philadelphia. I loved the rhythms of urban life, the constant activity that filled the streets, and the bars on every block that served Yuengling beer by the bucket-load. Even the refinery on I-76 almost looked inviting.

Senior year was a blur. I watched as my friends scrambled to find jobs or get accepted to graduate school. I celebrated when I heard they had been hired by a prestigious company or had gotten into medical school or law school. I knew what waited on the horizon for me, and I can't say I was looking forward to it. I was now finally enjoying college—the freedoms, the good-looking women, and all my friends—and I didn't want it to end. I was reading things that year that began to expand my mind and change the way I thought. I studied lots of theory and philosophy my last two semesters, reading Plato and Aristotle and Aquinas but also the modern critical thinkers like Derrida, Foucault, and Marx. I began to reread things I had read years earlier, amazed by how much my perspective had changed. After four years of college, I had only just begun to really feel that I was learning anything.

I was the battalion commander of the ROTC detachment at Drexel that year and spent as much time in the armory as I did anywhere else. I slept only a few hours every night, waking up at five in the morning to run with the other cadets for PT and then going to football practice at night. By the time I went to bed around one or two in the morning, I was exhausted. I was always either sick or recovering from illness, and the inhuman quantity of beer I was drinking on the weekends wasn't helping my health. Many nights I didn't even sleep, joining my best friend George for breakfast downtown in the early hours after morning PT and a full night spent in the library. He was hard at work on his senior thesis that fall semester, en route to graduate school at Harvard, and we prided ourselves on our "rigorous" intellectual lives and corresponding lack of sleep. Many of my friends openly worried that I was spreading myself too thin, but my grades were good, and I was determined to get the most out of college before my military service began. I went out of my way to join friends for coffee or drinks in the afternoons and on the weekends, enjoying their company while I could. I knew I wouldn't be around many people like my classmates once I joined the army.

Every so often, one of my friends would ask me why I was joining the army, and I always fumbled to find an answer. Back home, joining the military just seemed like a natural thing for a young man to do, even if not as many do it today as once did. (Still, even today, armed forces recruiting stations in the

South continue to fare far better than those in the North.) My friends at school, however, were forcing me to answer questions for myself as much as for them.

Why the hell *was* I joining the army? In a frighteningly short period of time, I would be a commissioned officer who could be leading men in combat. All that romantic crap I had thought in high school about being some sort of gun-toting tough guy didn't seem so valid anymore. But as I talked with my friends, I still could not imagine living to the age of sixty and looking back on a life in which I had never served. There was no war on the country's horizon in 2000, but I still felt that I should at least do my duty in the peacetime military.

My classical education helped to ease my doubts. In the polis of ancient Greece, it was the duty of every able man to serve in the military. The men of Athens and Sparta did not wait to be drafted under the threat of war. Instead, they grew up with the understanding that military service went hand-in-hand with citizenship. Taking up arms and learning military skills at a young age were facts of life for young Greeks. So if our society's culture of democracy had been built upon the Greek model, why should my classmates and I be any less ready to fight than the young men of Athens?

On May 20, 2000, just two days before I graduated with a double major in English and Classics, I was officially commissioned as a second lieutenant in the U.S. Army, Infantry. In three days, I would drive all my belongings back home to Chattanooga and set off cross-country to my first duty assignment, in Fort Lewis, Washington.

Now that college was over, the education of Andrew McDonald Exum could begin in earnest.

II

As I DROVE across the country to Fort Lewis, near Seattle, that summer, I had plenty of time to think about my new career. Despite the hundreds of hours of cadet training I had, I doubted whether I really knew how to be a soldier. There was no manual I could read to teach me to be *squared away*— army-speak for "highly competent and professional-looking." In my eyes, I was still a college student, not a defender of democracy. My new starched uniforms felt awkward on me, and for the first few months of my army career, I felt like I was playing a role rather than living a life.

That summer, the army had me working as a military journalist while I waited to go to the Infantry Officer Basic Course at Fort Benning, Georgia. When reporting as a "journalist" for the army, you quickly learn there is no news but good news. Writing for a weekly newspaper put out by U.S.

19

Army Cadet Command called the *Warrior Leader*, I put my Ivy League English degree to use writing shallow propaganda.

If I had to write a story on army cadets training at Fort Lewis, for example, my headline would read ARMY CADETS FIND FORT LEWIS TRAINING VALUABLE AND CHALLENGING. In reality, though, the training might be neither. (It certainly hadn't been when I went through the same course the summer before.) Or if I wrote a story on the regular army units supporting the summer training the cadets were going through, I would include only the positive quotes from soldiers, usually the officers, which might read something like: "We're all very excited to be training these cadets. This is an opportunity to train the future leaders of the army." I certainly would not include a very real and unscripted quote from a corporal or sergeant, which might read: "Pardon my French, sir, but this is bullshit. I need to be out training my guys, not some worthless fucking college kids."

The army got what they wanted from me, though—mainly because I made it a game to see just how falsely positive I could be. Reading the military articles of Second Lieutenant Andrew M. Exum, you would think the army was an idyllic organization comprised solely of tough, smart leaders and motivated soldiers. In my journalistic world, soldiers were "problem solvers," "positive thinkers," "cheerful" and "resourceful" volunteers. Morale problems were nonexistent. So too were racial tensions, adulterous soldiers, professional incompetence, and any of the other problems that often plague the modern military.

The army, of course, ate it up. At the end of the summer,

the Department of Public Affairs in Washington, D.C., named me one of the army's "Outstanding Journalists." I got a good laugh out of that, but the office where I worked gave me a pat on the back and a medal instead. I couldn't believe that I had earned my first medal from the army for writing in a news-paper.

All in all, Fort Lewis wasn't a bad experience. I traveled to Seattle more than a few times, Vancouver once, and Olympia a few times as well. I read a lot of books, and haunted the great Elliot Bay bookstore in Seattle, sweet-talking the girl at the counter with my over-inflected Tennessee accent while watch-ing all the punk rock kids and other disaffected Pacific North-west youth stroll by on the sidewalks of Pioneer Square. I also got into great shape that summer, working off all that beer I had drank in the final weeks of college, and I became fast friends with one of the other young officers I worked with.

Like me, Greg Darling was also an infantry officer and would be going to the same basic officer training course and on to Fort Drum in upstate New York as well. He was a trip. I knew, for example, that he was a born-again Christian who worshipped with one of the Pentecostal congregations in the area. But whenever we were off-duty, he wore combat boots, ripped jeans, and a dog collar, affecting the look of a genuine punk. Greg went to rock shows and raves on the weekend but never drank or used drugs. Despite the dark eyeliner he wore and safety pins on all his ripped T-shirts, I thought he was the most wholesome person I had ever met. He never even cursed. We went to a baseball game in Seattle that summer, and I can only imagine what we looked like sitting together, me in khakis, polo shirt, and Red Sox cap, Greg in some outrageous get-up and completely shaven head. We enjoyed each other's company, though, and looked forward to starting our infantry training together in the fall.

Yet I couldn't escape feeling that I was somehow doing less than the friends I had graduated college with. They were all either traveling in Europe that summer before beginning medical school, law school, or Ph.D. programs, or were already working, on their way to becoming the future business tycoons of America. For my part, I began to feel like I would be spinning my wheels during my four years in the army, doing a whole lot of nothing or writing senseless articles. It was a feeling I feared I would struggle with for my entire service in the military—that these upcoming years would be "lost" years in my life, years in which I would not accomplish anything of any value or substance. I felt that despite all the opportunities available in the world, I was stalling in the vast bureaucracy of the modern army.

But some words I came across that summer stood out among the dozen or so books I read during those ten weeks, and began to haunt me. In *The Last Gentleman*, Walker Percy wrote:

Southerners have trouble ruling out the possible. What happens to a man to whom all things seem possible and every course of action open? Nothing of course. Except war. If a man lives in the sphere of the possible and waits for something to happen, what he is waiting for is war—or the end of the world. That is why Southerners like to fight and make good soldiers. In war the possible becomes actual through no doing of one's own.

IT WAS AS IF Percy had been writing those words directly to me. I began to believe that war might be the only answer to all my doubts. That war might validate my existence as a soldier and a man.

As I DROVE back across the country that August, the West was going through some of the worst forest fires in recent decades. I-80 was a hazy strip of concrete and asphalt cutting through the walls of smoke. As I drove, I watched helicopters dip down into the Snake River and douse the fires with water just a few hundred meters off the four-lane highway. Somewhere in western Montana, I scribbled some verses down in my notebook with my right hand while holding the wheel between my left hand and my legs. I am too self-conscious of my amateur poetry to print those words, but the image that struck me that summer day was one of an army of flames advancing up those towering Montana hills. Driving in from Tennessee that June, I had never before seen a landscape as big as the Rockies, and now as I watched the fires rage while I stubbornly drove through the thick smoke, I wondered if God was somehow punishing the giant forests and mountains for their audacity to loom so large.

A few weeks after I left Fort Lewis, a pair of Arab terrorists detonated a bomb alongside the USS *Cole*, which was anchored in the Gulf of Aden. They claimed to do this in the name of God, against the American hegemony. The explosion killed nine U.S. servicemen, and in a war the United States did not yet realize it was fighting, first blood had been drawn.

III

IT WAS RAINING when we first formed up, never a good sign. The temperature was hovering around zero, and we were all, to a man, shivering with chills. We were the 240-odd members of United States Army Ranger School Class 4-01, gathered at Fort Benning, Georgia, and this was Day One of "Zero Week." This week was meant to acclimate Ranger candidates to the pressures of Ranger School. After five days, we would be given the weekend off before the *real* school began the following Monday.

The class was made up of soldiers, sailors, and airmen from all over the military, there to test themselves at what was widely considered to be the most physically demanding training course in the army, if not the entire military. The only schools I know that compare are the Navy Basic Underwater Demolitions Course—which trains future SEALs and frogmen—and the

25

air force's notoriously difficult pararescue course, which trains the men who rescue downed pilots.

The class was all male, of course, because women are excluded from most combat jobs, and it was comprised mostly of young soldiers from the army's three Ranger battalions and new second lieutenants like myself who had just completed the Infantry Officer Basic Course on the other side of Fort Benning. Because both the Rangers and the officer corps are mostly white, so was the class. Thrown into the mix were an assortment of marines, SEALs, Green Berets, air force PJs, and sergeants and officers from other light infantry battalions throughout the army.

Ranger School actually has nothing to do with the Army Ranger battalions under U.S. Army Special Operations Command, though all Rangers are required to complete the course in order to serve in those units. U.S. Army Ranger School is run by the Infantry School and is meant to test the endurance of small-unit leaders all over the military. Only trigger pullers need apply for admission. The school is designed to simulate the stress of combat on the soldiers who actually fight the nation's battles, not the support personnel and desk jockeys who comprise the majority of the military.

The first event of the first day was a physical fitness test. We marched over as a group and lined up outside a damp sawdust pit. The wind was awful when combined with the rain, and as we waited in lines to perform either push-ups, pull-ups, or sit-ups, we stood "nut to butt," pressed as close to one another as is humanly possible. I was grateful for the marine behind me who had no homophobic qualms about wrapping his arms around me. I figure this generous maneuver gave us both an extra five degrees of body warmth.

I cannot describe this kind of cold to those who've never experienced it. For most, extreme cold is transitory, something that is only experienced temporarily between locations of comfort. You're cold as you walk from your car to the shopping mall on a February afternoon or from your office across a windswept January street to a nearby deli. But many who have been in the military have experienced a different kind of cold. A cold that is *not* transitory. A cold for which there is not a light at the end of the tunnel, no warm department store a few hundred meters ahead, only more cold. I had felt this kind of cold before in the army, during the last few weeks of the Infantry Officer Basic Course in December, and it differed vastly from the cold I remembered from walking to class in the Philadelphia winter where I knew a warm classroom would be minutes away.

I lined up to do my push-ups. I had done forty-nine, the minimum, when the sergeant cut me off. I could have done more, but I had passed and that was all that mattered. The sergeant didn't feel like wasting time to see how many more I could do. The same thing went for the sit-ups. Once I had reached the minimum standard, the sergeant stopped me and sent me to the back of the line to prepare for the run. After the run—I took it easy to conserve my energy, ran with a friend, and came in at 13:30 for two miles—we did six pull-ups and were told to line up in formation to wait for the rest of the class to finish.

Once the physical fitness test was complete, we got onto the back of trucks bound for the pool, where we would undergo a combat water survival test. The instructors were looking to weed out weak candidates, spraying us with water hoses while we were on the side of the pool, urging us to quit, and looking for the slightest weakness or sign of panic in our swimming. The entire test was done in combat fatigues, so while swimming twenty-five meters may seem like a cinch, it can be difficult when done in heavy, soaking clothes, carrying full equipment and a rubber rifle. After the twenty-five-meter swim was complete, we were pushed off the high dive with a blindfold on and then, in the last event, were shoved under the water and had to ditch our gear before we resurfaced.

WE HAD DONE most of these events once already at the Infantry Officer Basic Course, a school that had unapologetically wasted the previous four months of my life. During the four months we spent at IOBC, most of the lieutenants drank every night and took little of the training seriously. The instructors were mostly bitter, over-the-hill sergeants who seemed to have one eye toward retirement and also seemed to resent the fact that they had to train cherry lieutenants fresh out of college. They treated us like privates, and for the most part, we responded by acting like them. I did learn some valuable lessons at IOBC, however, such as the one I got after the 2000 presidential election when one of my classmates told an instructor, a captain, that I had voted for Gore. The captain proceeded to lock me up at the position of attention and chew me a new asshole for not voting for Bush. I protested that I had voted for my Republican senator, but that wasn't enough evidently. All good officers, he told me, voted Republican, and Clinton had been responsible for all that was wrong with the military today. I could care less about that, really. I voted for Gore mainly because he was a Tennessean like me and my mother had always talked about what a great man his father had been.

What the officer had done was, in fact, illegal, but from that day forward I learned to keep my mouth shut when it came to politics. I had previously thought of myself as slightly conservative—at Penn I certainly could have been considered so—but the military was different. Most military folks are staunchly right-wing. But I wasn't offended. After all, as novelist Don DeLillo wryly notes, it often helps to "stick close to people in right-wing fringe groups." Their survival skills, as one might expect, are generally better than those of East Coast liberals. And—though many of my college classmates were serving the public as teachers or in other capacities—I didn't see many of those East Coast liberals serving alongside me in the military, so maybe the right-wingers in the Army at least had a sense of duty their liberal peers lacked.

My main gripe about Infantry Officer Basic Course was that—like most standard army training, including Basic Training—the standards for success were set too low. The instructors catered toward the lowest common denominator, pushing the training along at a slow and undemanding pace. Even the captain in charge of my platoon of lieutenants got frustrated with the poor quality of training, and responded by at least making the physical exercise he led us through as tough as possible. He also took time out at the end of the day to mentor us further than the training we received and let us know exactly what might be expected of us when we reached our first units as lieutenants.

What made Ranger School so welcome was that it didn't cater to the weakest student. The bar was set much higher, and the instructors counted on at least half the class being unable to handle the rigors of the course. The instructors advertised their job was to make our lives miserable for nineteen hours a day, with the other five hours reserved for eating, sleeping, and doing everything else we needed to do to stay alive. I was excited by the possibility of failure—it pushed me to be better and work harder to prepare. In theory, every infantry officer was required to attend Ranger School. I found, though, that you could easily tell those who really wanted to graduate from the course. We were the ones who had taken our preparation seriously during the basic course, lifting weights in the afternoons and running hard in the morning.

THOSE WHO DIDN'T pass the swim test or fitness test during Zero Week had a chance to retest during RAP Week, Ranger Assessment Phase, the first week of training. But we all knew that by the time you hit RAP Week, the instructors could drop you from the course for seemingly no reason at all as they looked to lower the number of students in the class. We had all heard horror stories of guys we knew who could do over a hundred push-ups in two minutes but somehow failed that event in the Ranger School PT test. So those of us who were serious all resolved to pass the PT test and water survival course the first time up. I did, but my buddy James didn't. I assured him he would pass it the next week, but he didn't and was shipped home early.

Most of my family has served as foot soldiers in the military, going all the way back to Colonel Benjamin Exum of the North Carolina militia during the American Revolution. I always tell people that my family has fought for the United States in every war—but one. In that war, I joke, "we wore gray and tried to kill as many Yankees as possible." As far as I can tell, though, Colonel Exum was the last one in my family to have been an officer. As a result, I chose the infantry as my branch to be the first Exum as an infantry officer since the Revolution.

I had been training for this school, really, for the past two years. That's when I resolved to become an infantry officer, and I knew that all infantry officers had to go to Ranger School. I also knew that officers who showed up to their units without Ranger tabs on their sleeves—the distinctive black and gold crescents worn on our left shoulders—were generally given the worst jobs. They were treated like failures from Day One at their new units. So even as I was finishing college, Ranger School had hung over my head like a gray cloud, following me wherever I went. I couldn't think about my future past Ranger School, and that's no joke. I knew I had the most challenging obstacle I would likely ever face in life just months ahead, and I worried about it constantly. For most soldiers, those months spent in Ranger School are the toughest ones they will ever live. We were told that the school itself physically took about seven years off your life.

When the school and my report date finally arrived, it was a relief. Since I had focused so much on Ranger School over the past few years and couldn't imagine the horror of leaving the school without my tab, I can honestly say that every day that I was at Ranger School, I didn't want to be anywhere else. Because being someplace else would have meant that I had either failed or quit. Being someplace else would have meant that I would soon head for Fort Drum to face a platoon of men without my Ranger tab and with little else to offer for credibility as a leader. (I had graduated from Infantry Officer Basic Course? So what.) But the black and gold Ranger tab worn on your uniform is a rare thing, even in infantry units. It's a universal sign of toughness and skill. It meant that, for at least a few months in your life, you had what it took to be squared away in some of the toughest conditions imaginable.

The rest of RAP Week was miserable. I vividly remember crawling through the notorious Malvestie Obstacle Course in the freezing rain. It was so cold the morning we went through that they had to break the thin layer of ice that covered the mud pit before we could pass through the course. Ranger instructors spit tobacco into the mud as we crawled under the barbed wire and through the thick, foul-smelling mire. I'll never forget what I felt when I hit that freezing mud for the first time. My body went into total shock. I gasped for air and felt my muscles freeze. Somehow I managed to start moving again, pulling myself through the mud and under the barbed wire of the course, my teeth chattering when not spitting out the mud that had gotten into my mouth. The RIs were yelling at us the entire time, hurling insults, telling us we were going too slow, that we were the most pathetic students they had ever seen, that we were worthless. After I had warmed up enough, I said to myself, *Fuck it,* and started to yell right back at the RIs. It was nothing insulting or even intelligible—I was just yelling at the top of my lungs in some wild primordial reflex. The guys next to me in the course began to laugh at me in between grunts and spits.

"Jesus fucking Christ, Ranger!" the RI yelled back at me. "I think you're fucking enjoying this!"

"Ahhh!!!" I responded. I figured that maybe if they thought I was crazy, they wouldn't fuck with me as much.

I definitely did *not* enjoy what immediately followed the obstacle course, when they wetted us down in the freezing air with a fire hose. It got the mud off but left our teeth chattering even worse afterward. My back muscles broke out in shivering spasms. All I wanted was a hot shower. Instead I got more push-ups and hazing.

The rest of the week was full of similar hazing and physical events. We did a land navigation test where within a time limit we had to find certain points in the woods with a map and compass, complete distance runs in full gear, and pass another timed five-mile run in order to stay in the course. We got three meals a day, which was a surprise, but we ate them in the chow hall with the RIs all yelling at us while we ate. You generally had about two minutes to eat everything on your plate, after which you were kicked out. You never got enough to eat, of course, and some guys ate their meals so quickly they threw up as soon as they left the chow hall. I felt especially sorry for those guys because I knew we needed as many calories as possible to keep our bodies from breaking down.

When we had no tests or training planned, they made us do push-ups, flutter-kicks, knee-benders, and every other conceivable callisthenic exercise, until we reached muscle failure—the point at which our muscles literally could not move our bodies anymore. I think I spent damn near that entire week at muscle failure. I remember not being able to do just ten freaking push-ups. I was that tired. I also perfected the art of "shamming," cheating the RIs by not doing the exercises when they looked the other way. I would drop a knee while doing push-ups or even contort my face into some grimace so that the RIs would think I was really reaching my physical limit when I actually had something left.

We did a lot of hand-to-hand combat training, but even that was used as an excuse to haze us. It was freezing outside, and during the night we were made to practice in pools of water and mud in the sawdust pit, rehearsing exotic throws and knife thrusts. None of this made any sense, really. To this day, when I find myself in a fight, I never use any of the complicated throws and parries they taught us in step-by-step fashion during Ranger School. But the end goal of the program was not to make us better fighters—it was to ingrain into us the spirit of the warrior, so that we were always ready to fight for our lives.

In a generation of kids raised on PlayStation, you have to teach young men to fight. It's not something most of us learn anymore as a matter of course, though I had been fortunate enough to have played enough football that physical aggressiveness came naturally to me. One of the challenges the army faces today is educating young men on how to be warriors, not in the Nintendo sense of the word, but in the visceral, primitive sense. It is one of the ironies of modern society that men have to rediscover their most base physical instincts, things ingrained in their psyches since our days as cavemen, in order to preserve a peaceful civilization. But the army's job is made tougher by a society in which young men are taught to apologize for their testosterone and aggressiveness. The military—and the infantry especially—remains one of the last places where that most endangered of species, the alpha male, can feel at home.

By the end of the week, we had lost about a third of our class. The last event was the twelve-mile foot march. Some guys' feet just couldn't take it. For others, pain—real, imagined, or invented—gave them an excuse to quit. We called these guys "Medical LOMs." LOM stood for Lack of Motivation, which was what they wrote on your evaluation report if you left the school under such circumstances. To leave Ranger School with an LOM on your record was a mark of shame. It meant you had quit of your own volition. The guys who pretended they were hurt or exaggerated their injuries made up medical reasons as an excuse to save face. We all saw through it, though. You could tell when guys were truly injured and when they were faking. We *all* hurt. We all had knocks, bruises, and strains. But as the Ranger Creed states, "Surrender is not a Ranger word." Those of us who made it learned to push past the pain. You couldn't ignore it—it hurt too damn much. You just had to learn to process the pain along with everything else and drive on toward your objective. That's the Ranger ethos, and it begins in Ranger School.

The beginning of the second week marked the beginning of the patrolling portion of the course, where we were taught to fight and conduct Ranger type missions (ambushes and raids) in the woods. This entailed being trucked from the main Ranger training camp to Camp Darby, a smaller camp deeper in the woods surrounding Fort Benning. Anyone who has seen a Vietnam war movie has a basic understanding of military patrolling—a group of soldiers stealthfully moving through the woods en route to an objective, constantly on the lookout for the enemy, wary of traps and ambushes. That's pretty much what we did in our missions at Ranger School, only, as with hand-to-hand combat, the most obvious reason for doing what we did was not the true one. Ranger School isn't meant to teach Rangers how to patrol—this is something we should have learned beforehand at our unit training. Ranger School is primarily a leadership course. Patrolling is just the way in which instructors evaluate the leadership skills of the candidates.

The hazing didn't stop when we arrived at Camp Darby, but all the Ranger candidates who had made it that far were by that time used to it. Between classes on how to conduct ambushes and reconnaissance, we ran through the Darby Queen Obstacle Course with our Ranger buddies and put on boxing gloves for boxing practice, which was part of our hand-to-hand combat training. Before we were allowed to box, the instructors made us do hundreds of push-ups and shoulder exercises, so that by the time we stepped into the ring we could barely raise our arms. This was intentional— the RIs didn't want anyone so strong he might hurt another student. If everyone was tired, they figured no one would get hurt. That didn't stop one Canadian soldier attending the course—on what was surely the world's cruelest exchange program—from knocking a West Point officer out with a right hook so vicious it caused him to be dropped from the course after emergency dental work. No doubt the Canadian was pissed off his army had shipped him off to such a torture session.

The classes were brutal. We sat in wooden bleachers and shivered throughout every class in the biting January chill. And if by chance we weren't cold at some point, it was impossible to stay awake because were only getting four hours of sleep a night at most. Usually we got only two or three. The RIs gave demerits to guys who fell asleep in class, and the demerits could cause you to fail the course. But even if you stayed awake, it was impossible to take notes. To take notes meant you had to take off your gloves, and the muscles in your hands don't respond like they're trained to when they're cold. I still have my Ranger Handbook from when I went through the course, and you can tell what notes I took in Benning and what notes I took later on in Florida. The notes from Florida Phase are written in my normal, neat handwriting. By comparison, the notes I took at Benning look like chicken scratch. I couldn't help it. My fingers were just too damn cold and either shivered ferociously or moved in comical slow motion whenever I tried to write.

When we finally began patrolling, our squad was a disaster. For some squads, patrolling at Darby is easy—everyone is disciplined and works together. My squad, however, was a mess. Guys fell asleep on patrol, guys wouldn't run when they needed to, guys forgot things they had been told by their leaders. Each member of the squad rotated through different leadership positions. The RIs walked with us, evaluating each leader. Each of us had to pass a leadership position in order to advance to the next phase. My own leadership opportunities were nightmares. Once, one of the guys in my team got caught eating when he was supposed to be on guard. The asshole had just passed *his* patrol and was relaxing at my expense. I was furious. By the time we completed our patrols, we all knew we had faired poorly.

The only thing left in the phase was the peer evaluations, where each member of the squad rated every other member of his squad. After those were completed, we were all called into the small shed the RIs used and told individually whether we had passed or not. As I expected, my squad did horribly. More than half of us—including me—had failed and would have to start this phase of Ranger School over. I took some comfort in the fact that my squad had rated me the best Ranger in the peer evaluations, but I dreaded the prospect of doing everything over again all the same.

Some guys quit right there, once they were told they had been recycled. Quitting wasn't an option for me, despite the physical wreck my body was. I couldn't imagine the horror of reporting to my unit at Fort Drum without my Ranger tab.

Recycling the phase wasn't that bad, really. They let us eat as much as we wanted before the next phase was scheduled to begin, and after some deliberation, they decided we wouldn't have to complete RAP Week again—we could start over with patrols. They also looked the other way when people from the outside sent us reading material and goodies in the mail. Normally any reading material outside the Bible or the Ranger Handbook was taboo at Ranger School, but I vividly remember reading Maugham's *The Razor's Edge* during one week I spent as a recycle. Maugham's narrative of expatriates in post–World War I Paris had a devastating effect on me—for the rest of the school, I had an insatiable craving for beer and scrambled eggs. I also got through the first fifty or so pages of Kant's *Critique of Pure Reason*, but Kant proved too weighty a tome to tackle while recovering in the barracks at Ranger School (or any time since, for that matter). Instead I opted to read the contraband *Playboys* my buddy in the next bunk had acquired.

Midway through my first week as a recycle, one of the RIs discovered my secret talent, which would doom me for the rest of my days spent waiting for the next course to begin. I had perfected my skill with a floor buffer the summer before in Fort Lewis with Greg. Because we had been the lowest-ranking officers in the office, we had to clean up every night. We would often mount the industrial floor buffers and ride them in our "Office Buffer Rodeo Challenge," laughing as we flew across the room and into the walls long after the rest of the office had left for the evening. We made it a game to see who could sit on the spinning buffer the longest.

One night at Ranger School, I was asked to buff the RI offices. The next morning, I was called in to speak to the sergeant in charge. He pointed to the gleaming floor.

"Did you do that?" he asked.

I looked down at my reflection in the shiny floor, then back at him. "Roger, Sergeant."

"That's fucking awesome, Ranger," he said. "But you realize you've fucked yourself, right?"

"Um, roger, Sergeant."

I would buff the floors not only of that office but of brigade headquarters every night from that moment on until my stint as a recycle ended. By the time the next class started, I was desperate to get back to the grueling training again rather than continue buffing every floor in the camp each night.

I made some great friends as a recycle, though, including a Green Beret from Fort Lewis, who had hurt his knee in Darby, as well as an artillery officer from Fort Drum named Brad who had graduated from Williams College in Massachusetts. The three of us were in the same squad the second time through Darby, and we joked that we were the best educated machine gun team in the U.S. Army. I also made friends with the RIs, not only through my skill as a floor waxer but also through the impressions I had cultivated of the other RIs. I have always had a gift for impressions. In the Infantry Officer Basic Course, my platoon had won the skit contest as a result of my impressions of our platoon trainer. At Ranger School, I had the RIs rolling with laughter every time they had me imitate another instructor.

BRAD AND I linked up with our new patrolling squad immediately after they finished RAP Week. My new Ranger buddy, Isaac, was a recent West Point graduate from rural Illinois who had been forced to recycle the course in its entirety after a can of tobacco was discovered in his rucksack. He would make me renounce almost every bad thing I had ever said about West Point graduates (and I had said plenty). Isaac was okay by anyone's standards, a tough German whose family had fought on both sides of the last world war. By the time we reached Florida phase of Ranger School, we would joke that we were the two "old men" of the class. Every military school that tests the limits of human endurance assigns each student a "buddy," and as Ranger buddies, Isaac and I would never leave each other's side during the next few months, doing virtually everything together, never letting each other get out of arm's length.

In contrast to our previous squads, this one worked extremely well together, and patrolling went a lot better the second time around. We all got along well, and I was even able to help some of the guys with their patrols because this was my second time around. I passed relatively easily. Even the other parts of the phase seemed easier the second time around. In my thirty-second boxing match, I knocked the headgear off my opponent. I couldn't see too well through my own headgear, so I just kept on punching. I felt bad, but the kid was okay, and we shook hands afterward. A few of us recycles turned the Darby Queen Obstacle Course into a game. We laughed off the RI taunts and insults, and once they saw they couldn't shake us, they began to laugh at our jokes as well, while we worked our way through the maze of obstacles.

One thing that didn't change was the hunger we constantly experienced. We figured we ate about two thousand calories a day, but due to the cold and all the physical activity we did, we were probably burning closer to three thousand. Our thick, muscled bodies quickly turned to skin and bones. At night, I watched as Ranger students sneaked off to the Dumpster behind the camp, where they would dive into the garbage with red-lens flashlights in search of food the RIs had thrown away. Soon, we all were volunteering for garbage detail on the off chance that we might find an uneaten cracker or package of peanut butter lying in the trash.

By the second week of Darby Phase, we all knew how many calories were in every single item in every variation of the MRE (Meal, Ready to Eat). We traded the items among ourselves, not based on how well each item tasted, but rather on how filling each item was.

I'VE NEVER BEEN so happy as when I got on the bus to advance to Mountain Phase. I remember the bitter envy I had felt when I saw the rest of my original class advance a few weeks earlier while I sat outside the recycle barracks. This time around, I watched out the windows of the bus as others sat watching us from the same place I had been almost a month ago.

On the bus ride up to Dahlonega, Georgia, the RIs pretty much left us alone and let us relax. They passed out the mail that had arrived for us in the past few weeks, including the packages our relatives had sent containing junk food and goodies. We greedily munched on all the stuff we had been sent, frustrated that we couldn't eat any more than our shrunken stomachs would allow. The bus ride was only four hours, and we had a limited time to eat and sleep in peace. Most guys ate until they were stuffed and then passed out.

I ate until I was stuffed, drank some water, and ate some more. I was ravenous and knew that the minute we arrived in Dahlonega, the RIs in Mountain Phase would confiscate all our food. Lord only knew when they would feed us next. By this point I had learned to take very little for granted.

GEORGIA MAY SEEM like an unusual setting for the Mountain Phase of Ranger School, but the Appalachian Mountains of the northeast part of the state are perfect, mainly because the climate offers year-round training. In the first week of the phase, we were taught knots, basic climbing and rappelling skills, and the types of equipment we might need in mountainous terrain.

The hazing stopped for the most part once we arrived in the mountains. The Mountain Phase RIs figured we were all at least somewhat competent after surviving their peers at Darby Phase, so they concentrated more on teaching us rather than trying to get us to quit. We trained out of Camp Frank D. Merrill in Dahlonega, aside from the few days we spent atop Mount Yonah, climbing routes and learning intermediate climbing skills. I had climbed all my life in the mountains around this area, so most of the training was easy for me and generally boring. I spent most of my time helping others with their equipment and with finding the elusive handholds on their assigned routes.

During the course of the first week, one of the seams in my pants busted from all the rugged activity, and when one of the RIs knelt down to check my climbing harness, he was shocked to discover that one of my testicles had slipped through the busted seam and now stared at him inches away from his face.

"For fuck's sake, Ranger!" he yelled, leaping back.

My squad and I bent over with laughter, and I made a mental note to sew up the seam later that night.

The field portion of Mountain Phase consisted of two five-day missions in the woods along the Tennessee Valley Divide. The treks up and down the TVD were torturous, especially when we were each saddled with ninety pounds of equipment. By this point we had put four squads together and were training as a platoon. Our platoon worked even better together than our squads had separately, and we all did well patrolling despite the often harsh elements.

The cold—not hunger or lack of sleep—was our worst enemy in the mountains. We dreaded the sunset, because nighttime meant a drastic drop in the temperature. We began to "spoon" with each other every night, lying down together and huddling close, with our poncho liners over the top of us. Spooning isn't for the homophobic, but I've observed that few guys are when they're soaking wet and the temperature is zero degrees. The desire to be warm usually trumps machismo. I remember hiking up the TVD one day in a rainstorm that turned to snow as soon as we crested the ridge. We were thoroughly soaked by nightfall, and two guys contracted hypothermia by the next morning and were dropped from the course. Three others quit outright before daybreak.

At another point during a field problem, we were all—to a man—soaked to the bone in below-freezing temperatures and without a single piece of dry clothing among us. The RIs made the call at that point to extract us from the mountains in order to let us use the dryers at camp for a few hours before we began training again. As recently as fifteen years ago, the RIs would not have allowed us to do that and would have taken the risk that many of us might catch pneumonia. But after four Ranger students died in Florida Phase in the early 1990s, the RIs have taken more rigorous safety precautions. A few times, the temperature dropped so low at night that the RIs allowed us to build fires. Of course, building fires out of waterlogged deadfall is a challenge at best, but that was our problem. Once the fires were built, the next task was keeping everyone awake to pull security and keep the fires going. I watched one guy fall asleep one night standing up by a fire, falling facedown into the embers before we picked him back up, his face slightly burned and covered with soot. He later quipped this was the only time he felt warm the entire phase.

The remainder of Mountain Phase passed without much event, aside from the mild frostbite that struck the tips of my ears. After the numbness subsided, they began peeling and hurting like hell. The RIs were as grossed out as I was in pain, so they let me wear my black wool knit cap over my ears to protect my ears as well as their eyes. Our platoon performed superbly despite the elements. Every single one of us advanced to the final phase, Florida Phase, even though the weather had been horrific throughout our stay in Dahlonega.

On the way out of our last patrol in Mountain Phase, a buddy and I—feeling happy about the fact that we had just passed the phase—decided to harass the helicopter pilots giving us a ride by passing up a note written on a three-by-five index card that read, in bold, black block letters: YOU FLY LIKE A GIRL. The pilots responded by giving us the ride of our lives, arching and diving through the Appalachian Mountains of northeast Georgia until every Ranger student on the bird was either green with motion sickness or yelling at the top of his lungs from fear.

We didn't get the same opportunity to chow down on our packages after Mountain Phase as we had after Darby Phase. Guys had to throw hundreds of dollars' worth of food their parents, wives, and friends had sent into the Dumpster because our class was running behind schedule and had to catch a bus to an airbase north of Atlanta in order to fly to Florida Phase. We were bitter about losing our packages, but the excitement of advancing to the final phase of Ranger School was more than enough to make up for our disappointment.

IV

Florida Phase of Ranger School is conducted in the backwoods of Eglin Air Force Base in the Florida Panhandle. Also called "Swamp Phase" because of the terrain, Florida Phase taught me the most about how to be a platoon leader. Once at Fort Drum, I knew, I would inherit a platoon filled with guys who already knew how to patrol. Florida Phase would provide me with a number of different ways to "crack the nut," and I knew the knowledge I would accumulate there would empower me in my new job.

Florida Phase is built around one nine-day field problem, preceded by a few days of classroom instruction. The instruction was the best thus far because the instructors treated us like adults and—more importantly—peers. They all knew that the vast majority of the students who had advanced this far would graduate, and the RIs were trying to teach us as many

47

new things as possible to take back to our units. Of course, we still had to pass our patrols, and patrolling Florida was as tough as anywhere.

During the course of the field problem, we would receive a new mission every morning in our patrol base, plan all morning, move during the afternoon to our objective, attack at nightfall, and move to our new patrol base at night, arriving at midnight or later depending on how well the mission had gone and how well the point man navigated through the swamps and woods. We worked in the patrol base for about an hour at night, only to wake up early the next morning—assuming we got any sleep at all—for the new mission. Regardless of whether we had slept or not the night before, we had plenty to do the next day. The platoon's leadership switched out every morning along with the RIs who walked with us.

We went for as long as forty-eight hours without any food and rarely got more than an hour and a half of sleep each night. Because of it, I almost killed Isaac as we dug into our positions one night.

I was digging our foxhole while he pulled security in the patrol base after a mission, but he was so exhausted that he literally could not stay awake for more than ten seconds at a time. I tried everything to keep him awake long enough for me to dig both our positions—kicking him, punching him, hitting him with my shovel. But every time, he would wake up, not remember a thing, and angrily ask why I was hitting him over the head with my entrenching tool.

The guys in our squad joked about "Exum's Four Phases of Anger." If I caught someone sleeping while on security, I would first only shake him and admonish him to stay awake. If

I caught that person sleeping a second time, though, I would be harsher, telling him to stand on a knee to keep awake. If I caught a person sleeping a third time, I would get full-blown angry, usually getting in his face and yelling something eloquent, along the lines of "Hey, motherfucker! Stay the fuck awake!" And if I caught someone sleeping a fourth time, it was game on. My fists would start flying. As my fists and elbows became a blur of motion, my squad mates would just sit back and watch the show, keeping an eye out for any Ranger instructors who might be lurking in the tree line. Usually, whoever was the platoon leader positioned me with one of the guys who couldn't stay awake. They knew I would keep him awake, or at least bruise my knuckles trying.

That same night that I was beating Isaac with my entrenching tool, a night in which I was as sick as I could be of my squad and desperately wanted time alone, it rained horribly. The lightning at Eglin Air Force Base is famous for its intensity, and the instructors made us leave all our equipment in our holes. We gathered in the center of the patrol base, away from anything metallic, and the RIs told us they were going to let us sleep without interruption for a good three hours if we could stand the rain long enough to doze off. The rain, however, was warmer than the freezing rain in northeast Georgia, so I fell into an uneasy sleep immediately, with the rain pounding on my flimsy jacket. I was sick of my squad, sick of the school, and only wanted to rest for just a while in peace, weather be damned. A few minutes into my rest, though, Oz, the youngest member of the squad, woke me up and told me to follow him. Oz had discovered a flat tree stump a few inches off the ground.

"I figure if you lay one way, and I lay the other way," he said, "we can both put our heads on this stump and use it for a pillow. Who knows? Maybe we'll sleep better."

Six days into the field problem, nearly everyone was thinking only of himself. Yet Oz had gotten himself up in the pouring rain, walked over to where I was and clued me in to the nearby stump because he figured such a good pillow would be a shame for only one person to use. I know this seems such a ridiculous and small thing, but Oz damn near brought tears to my eyes with his kindness. The two of us slept soundly for the next few hours, our heads leaning against each other and propped up by the soggy tree stump.

Oz's lesson was that kindness and charity toward your fellow Ranger is a rare and good thing indeed when you're tired and hungry and haven't showered in ten days. And it was a reminder that we all needed each other if we were to have any hope for passing the course. I resolved then to not let the school get the best of me, to continue helping everyone pass the course. Because I had demonstrated a talent for writing operations orders, I helped almost everyone in the platoon write his during Florida Phase. On one mission, I was chosen to be the platoon leader. I had no way of knowing it at the time, but I had already passed the course. They gave me another patrol to give all the guys under me—my squad leaders and platoon sergeant—a better chance of passing as well. They figured I could make things go smooth enough to allow the others the best chance for a "go" on their patrol. Sure enough, the patrol went off without a hitch and all those guys passed.

The walk out of Florida Phase remains to this day the

most painful thing I have ever done. Our feet were all soaked from nine days spent walking around in the swamps. The leather insoles of my jungle boots had long rotted out, and I was starting to develop blisters on both of my feet. For the first few miles of the walk, we were on sand. Isaac and I were carrying one of the machine guns, him with the gun itself and me with the twenty-pound tripod on my back in addition to all my other gear. The minute we hit the asphalt, the skin on the bottom of my feet rubbed off just enough to create enormous, Oreo cookie–sized blisters on both my feet, which I would walk on, with tears in my eyes, for the next seven miles into the base.

When we arrived at the base, they told us to strip off our gear so they could weigh us. Isaac helped me get my boots off and then carried me onto the scales as if I had two broken legs.

"Jesus. What's your problem, Ranger?" the RI said with genuine concern.

I showed him the bottom of my swollen, blistered feet.

"Jesus," he said again, shaking his head in sympathy.

I weighed 160 pounds on the scale, thirty-four less than I had when I started the course. Isaac and I got some fresh socks on my feet along with new boots, and I was able to stumble around for the next two days by walking very, very slowly. The next day, I visited the medic's station, where they drained two full syringes of bloody fluid from my two feet.

But first came the moment of truth when they told us whether or not we had passed the course. In the end, half of our platoon in Florida had not. Only four guys in my squad had—two buddy teams, Isaac and me and Sean and Oz. The four of us had worked well together the whole course, and we would enjoy the trip back to Georgia while the rest of our squad stayed in Florida to recycle the phase. We felt as awful for our mates as we felt elated at our own success, so we kept quiet that night, sharing all the food we had been sent with the guys we would be leaving behind.

Within a few days, we all boarded a C-130 to fly back to Fort Benning, where we parachuted onto the base's main drop zone just over the state line in Alabama. I hit a wet patch and got dragged through a foot of water by my parachute before I could disconnect my risers and deflate the chute. I was soaked but didn't care, even when Isaac and my squad mates openly laughed at me in the assembly area.

When we got back to the Fort Benning Ranger Camp, they gave us a night off, and we were allowed to go into town if we wanted to. We had all heard the horror stories of Rangers about to graduate getting drunk and getting thrown out of the course just prior to graduation, so we decided to take it easy. None of us had been allowed any tobacco during the course, and even though I almost never smoke or dip, Isaac and I went through two whole packs of Marlboro Reds that night. We had been talking about how good a cigarette would taste all throughout the school and smoked like chimneys the first chance we got. We also ate an entire pizza, each, and Oz and I somehow had the energy and willpower to split a pint of ice cream between the two of us afterward. After starving for so long, I was determined to get fat on all this junk food.

In the next few days, as our parents came through town and took us all out to dinners and lunches in their efforts to make us look healthy again, they would make the mistake of asking the other guys in the squad out as well. I think Oz and I damn near bankrupted Sean's parents one night we ate so much.

GRADUATION FROM RANGER School was one of the best days of my life, and if you ask any other Ranger, he'll tell you the same thing. Half my family made the three-hour drive from home. My mother and father and grandmother and cousin and aunt and uncle were all there. My father pinned my Ranger tab onto my sleeve with tears in his eyes. He was proud of me and happy to see me in one piece, at least until he saw where the tip of my frostbitten ear had once been. Ranger School goes to great lengths to make graduation a really big deal, so we all sat through a huge demonstration by the Ranger instructors and a speech by some big-shot colonel.

My father sent me an e-mail the following day, saying how much the graduation had meant to him. He said he had never been more proud of me in his whole life and that I was everything he had always wanted me to be.

To his credit my father has always been wary of fathers who try to live their dreams out through their sons. As a sportswriter, he had seen plenty of young athletes ruined by their overbearing fathers. So he never pressured me when it came to athletics. I never gave a hint that I might be a star athlete, though, so that probably helped him keep his mind level regarding sports and me.

The military was a different thing entirely. My father was always buying me books about navy SEALs and marines when I was a kid, partly because he saw I had an interest and partly because he himself was interested. I think my father has always suffered a lot of guilt from Vietnam. His older brother Kinch had gone and served proudly as a marine on the front lines for two tours. But he had never been the same since, racing stock cars on dirt tracks and working odd jobs on his return. Though she herself was only a few years old when Uncle Kinch shipped off, my aunt has a framed picture of him as a nineteen-year-old marine infantryman up in her house and has told me that she considers the day he left for Vietnam the day he died. The man who came back just wasn't the same boy who'd left.

I have only heard one story from someone who actually saw Kinch during the war, so it's tough to tell what my uncle went through. A friend of my father's, however—another marine—was heading north on Highway One near the demilitarized zone one afternoon when a voice began to shout his name from the side of the road. It was my uncle, almost unrecognizable, thin and covered in reddish mud from head to toe. The truck my father's friend was on sped up, though, and aside from that passing glimpse they never saw each other again until after the war.

My father, however, never served. I do not know whether my father wanted to go. The family had other things planned for him, and never even let the possibility of going enter his head. He was the golden boy of the family, the one everyone pinned hopes on, and the family did everything they could to keep him from going the way his older brother had. His aunt, a doctor, wrote a statement that he had an ulcer. And Kinch himself had enlisted for a second tour, which would have changed Dad's draft status because one member of the family was already serving.

So while thousands of other young Tennesseans were drafted, fought, and died, my father stayed home and helped run the family newspaper. I know the knowledge that some-one served in his place kills him at night. I know it pains him that while others were toiling in the single defining event of their generation, Dad was driving from town to town covering college football games and drinking beer with his buddies.

So having a son in the military—one who had graduated from Army Ranger School no less—meant the world to my fa-ther. He has always been horrified by the possibility of me getting shot at or dying in combat—as you would expect any parent to be—but he has always loved the fact that I decided to serve. In a way, I fulfilled all my mother's dreams for me by graduating from Penn and validating all her hard work spent raising me. By becoming a Ranger, I would similarly fulfill my father's aspirations.

I had gone into the military and into Ranger School with a theory about myself, a theory that I could be just as tough as the guys on the recruiting poster and perhaps even tougher. I imagined I could be just as good a soldier as my grandfather or my uncle, and even better, and dreamed that I could be-come a member of one of the great military elites of my day. When I got older, I would be able to tell my son what I had been and what I had done with no small amount of personal pride.

I proved my theory. I had acquitted myself just as honor-ably as I had hoped. I couldn't see myself as any different than when I had reported on Day One. I just knew myself better, and that alone gave me a fresh burst of confidence. Whereas once I had a vague notion of the kinds of pain I could endure, the exhaustions I could face, I now knew much better my own personal limits, physical and mental. I discovered that I could push my body and my spirit far beyond what I would have previously thought possible. What that knowledge firmly in my head, I prepared to face what was perhaps an even greater test. I prepared to face the men I would be asked to lead into combat.

V

DRIVING NORTH ON I-81 from Tennessee is one of the prettiest drives in the United States. Leaving Bristol, you work your way through the hills of southwest Virginia until you spill into the picturesque Shenandoah Valley, where General Stonewall Jackson defeated four Union armies with a small band of sixteen thousand men in the Civil War. Then you drive through picturesque slices of West Virginia and Maryland before hitting the farms of southern Pennsylvania where General Robert E. Lee terrorized the North before being routed at Gettysburg, just off to the right of the interstate.

But once you drive north of Harrisburg, Civil War history no longer applies to the landscape and you instead find yourself in the hills and mountains of eastern Pennsylvania and New York. Some romantic pioneers named the cities north of Binghamton after places in antiquity like Marathon and

Ithaca, and the surrounding landscape of small farms and green hills has a warm, wholesome feeling about it. Far from the rough edges of New York City to the southeast, the people you meet on the way are nice and helpful, eager to start a conversation or inquire where you're coming from and where you're going.

North of Syracuse, the terrain grows unremarkable and flat. In the winter, the dry, wide fields look like frozen tundra, devoid of character and life. The people here are as bored with their home as any visitor, and most of the young people in the area flee to Syracuse or beyond once they can finish high school. You can almost sense the impatience of the other drivers on I-81, eager to either cross over into Canada or make it to the Thousand Islands region to fish and relax on vacation. There is nothing of consequence here, nothing at all worthwhile in the "Northcountry" as the locals call it.

Nothing, except for Fort Drum.

Fort Drum lies on a stretch of flat, swampy land in upstate New York wedged between Lake Ontario and the Canadian border. The weather is notoriously harsh in the winters, when the temperature regularly dips to negative thirty degrees Fahrenheit and the snowdrifts often measure above six feet thanks to the "lake effect" of easterly winds gathering speed and moisture as they pass over Lake Ontario. It seems unusual that a unit named the Tenth Mountain Division would be located at a place so low in altitude, but a combination of politics and a lack of common sense destined otherwise.

The construction of Fort Drum initially began as a scheme to invigorate a depressed section of northern New York, isolated from major cities by distance and weather. Watertown, a grumpy little hamlet of around forty thousand located seventy miles north of Syracuse, is the closest city to the base, though several smaller towns surround the post. When the army looked to add another major military installation as well as another light infantry unit in the military buildup of the 1980s, Fort Drum was chosen after shrewd political haggling on the part of area congressmen. The base did its part to invigorate the region economically, but to hear some of the locals tell it, the area was better off before the army moved in.

The Tenth Mountain Division—a unit that had not been active since the Second World War—was chosen to populate Fort Drum as a sort of thank-you note to Senator Bob Dole, a decorated veteran of the division in that war. This, however, was not Senator Dole's Tenth Mountain Division, a unit comprised originally of the best backcountry skiers and mountaineers to be found in the United States, including Olympic medalists and European champion skiers, one of whom was the world record holder in the ski jump. In 1945, the division mounted a series of daring assaults on German positions in the Italian Alps, scaling cliffs at night by hammering in pitons in pitch-black darkness, with socks over their hammers to muffle the noise. The new Tenth Mountain Division, by contrast, was a plain-vanilla light infantry unit, specializing in shooting and walking long distances with obscene amounts of equipment on their backs. Nothing about the unit maintained any connection with the old traditions or with the designation as a "mountain" unit aside from the base's street signs named after the division's famous World War II victories at Riva Ridge and Mount Belvedere.

I had originally been attracted to Fort Drum because the

Tenth Mountain Division was currently the most deployed unit in the army. The Tenth had been to Somalia, Haiti, Bosnia, the Sinai, and Kosovo in recent years. Plus, soldiers in the Tenth were known to be tough, and hardened by a combination of the brutal weather around Watertown and the "real world" deployments.

The unit defied the traditional demographics of the largely Southern American army. Because of its status as the only major army base in the northeast, a larger percentage of the soldiers at Fort Drum were from relatively nearby urban areas like Boston and New York. And this being the army, many of these soldiers were minorities—blacks and Hispanics—which come to think of it may have been the reason why so many of the homogenous Northcountry locals objected to the post and its soldiers. As one local confessed to me, Watertown did not have a single black resident until the army came to town.

I arrived at Fort Drum at the end of April 2001, about two weeks after I graduated from Ranger School. For a full week after graduation, I had carried a bag of granola and M&Ms everywhere I went, in a largely successful effort to gain back all the weight I had lost. I arrived at Fort Drum bloated and out of shape but happy to start my duties with my new unit. If I did well at Drum, I might even have the opportunity to serve as a senior lieutenant in one of the elite Ranger battalions.

Fort Drum is one of the most modern military bases, being one of the newest, but once you leave the post, the economic realities of the surrounding communities hit you hard. Crumbling farmhouses and old textile mills dot the landscape around Watertown. Like all officers and sergeants, I could be quartered off the base, and I quickly found a small apartment in the lakeside community of Sackets Harbor, about a twenty-five-minute drive west of the post.

I arrived at a good time in the year, just as things were beginning to thaw. There was still frost on my windshield every morning, but for the most part the weather was nice. In the summers the Thousand Island region along the St. Lawrence River becomes a vacation spot for Northerners and Southerners alike looking to escape the heat of the summer, and tiny lakeside communities like Sackets Harbor were already gearing up for the influx of "summer people."

I was apprehensive about meeting my battalion and company commanders on my third day at Drum. My battalion commander, I soon learned, was a well-liked and respected officer who had spent most of his career in the elite Ranger units. To a young lieutenant such as myself, Colonel Matthews was highly intimidating. Thin and intense, he looked every bit like the renowned distance runner he was. We went for a run following my introduction, and three miles in I realized that I would have to get into much better shape if I ever expected to keep up on runs with my new battalion commander.

That morning I met my company commander as well as the platoon leader I would soon replace. A light infantry rifle company consists of three rifle platoons and a six-man mortar section. Each platoon has a platoon leader, usually a lieutenant, with a captain in command of the company. The commander also has an executive officer who serves as the second-in-command and is usually an experienced former platoon leader about to become a captain himself. Bobby, the lieutenant I would replace, was the only Ranger-qualified platoon leader in the company, and one of only four Ranger-qualified soldiers, enlisted or officer, out of the 120 men in the company. This came as a shock to me as Isaac had sent word from Fort Bragg that his *platoon* in the 82nd Airborne Division had no less than twelve Ranger-qualified soldiers and sergeants. In my new platoon, I was jokingly referred to as "The Lone Ranger."

But everyone in the company said my platoon, "The Gladiators," was among the best in the battalion. Sergeant Montoya, my new platoon sergeant, was highly regarded as well. I got a chance to meet him when Bobby took me to my new office. Sergeant Montoya sat in the desk facing the one that would be mine. He was a bald-headed man of thirty-four with a handshake like a vise grip and dark, wide eyes that had seen most of what there was to see in the army. I usually can't tell much about people when I first meet them, but I immediately had the feeling that Sergeant Montoya was the kind of consummate professional that perpetually kept the army from plunging into chaos. I liked him instantly and felt lucky to have him around to keep me out of trouble.

After just a few weeks, our company commander took another job with a different company, and we received a new commander. A diminutive man with thick glasses, our new commander looked like the type of guy who got picked on a lot in high school. As we soon found out, however, Captain John Rogers had both a compact athletic build and an aggressive personality to complement his sharp intellect. I had heard Captain Rogers described as alternately abrasive and funny, but I decided to withhold judgment until I knew him better. All I knew about him at first was that he was the fastest man in the battalion, able to run ten miles in less than an hour.

To my surprise and delight, Greg Darling, the punk rocker I had served with at Fort Lewis the summer prior, joined my company as one of the other two platoon leaders. I had known he was coming to Fort Drum like me, but I figured the odds were stacked against the two of us being in the same battalion, let alone the same company. He was now engaged to be married to his girlfriend, Faith, a beautiful girl he had shown me pictures of in Seattle. In every picture he had shown me, she had a different color hair—pink in one picture, green in another, blond in yet another. She would travel with Greg to punk shows in New York City and Boston on weekends. I went south to their wedding in Binghamton, New York, a few weeks later, where they both cleaned up enough to look highly presentable in the church. Bald-headed Greg, wearing tails, looked like Billy Corgan in the Smashing Pumpkins's "Tonight, Tonight" video. Both of their fathers were ministers and officiated at the ceremony. They recessed to a punk rock song, making it one of the oddest, best weddings I have ever attended.

It wasn't long before I got into the scheme of things at Fort Drum. Bobby was becoming the mortar platoon leader, so I moved all his stuff into the hallway and moved all my stuff into the office. The work we were required to do really wasn't that difficult. Sergeant Montoya handled most of the day-to-day operations in the platoon, leaving me to plan training with the other officers. I worked on getting myself back into shape, foolishly running twice a day until I developed painful shin splints that would take me a full year to recover from.

Our executive officer was a lieutenant like me who was a fitness nut, a triathlete who got me cycling on a regular basis to supplement my running regimen.

We left the office for my first training exercise with the platoon a few weeks after I arrived, driving on five-ton trucks into the woods of Fort Drum. We did close-quarters marksmanship exercises, practicing shooting targets rapidly at close range, and then did a squad live fire exercise where my men advanced through the woods with live rounds in their weapons and engaged targets that popped up when I pressed a button on the remote control box. Live fire exercises are the closest approximation to combat, as they require soldiers to move and react, shooting live rounds while their leaders make decisions on how to shift them around on the battlefield. Though I knew enough to make some intelligent criticisms, as the new guy I mostly listened to what my sergeants and commander had to say during the evaluations that followed each exercise.

I got on easily with my sergeants and the rest of the platoon. Without much to do aside from watch my squads train, I hung out with Sergeant Montoya and walked around to where my guys lounged between their turns in the exercise. As with my sergeants, I mostly kept quiet and asked a question here and there with my men at first. I knew most of them did not have the background I did, and I wanted to know where they came from. Most of them were nineteen or twenty, so I was able to joke about the same things they did, alluding to the same rap stars or movies.

I sensed a wariness, though, and felt when I was alone in the center of the rest of the platoon, that all eyes were on me, watching to see what I did, how I conducted myself. Some of the guys were more outgoing than others and asked me questions, like where I had gone to school, where I was from, and how tough Ranger School was. I didn't want to dwell on where I went to college, fearing the men would see me as some sort of stuck-up elitist, so I spoke with a stronger than usual Tennessee accent and talked more about home than I would have normally. Most of the men seemed to understand that better, and it made them feel more comfortable dealing with a guy from the South instead of an Ivy League graduate. When we did talk about where I went to school, we mostly talked about the basketball team. The men said I should join them for a pickup game when we returned to base, and I agreed.

The afternoon before we left on the exercise, I got up from where I had been sitting with Sergeant Montoya and walked over to a large boulder, where I took a leak. When I had buttoned up my pants and turned around, I saw that the platoon had crept up en masse and gathered around me.

I have been in enough fights to know when I am in trouble, and I saw immediately that I was about to receive my unofficial initiation into the platoon. The first soldier who attacked me I wrestled to the ground and held close to protect the front of my body. The rest of the platoon piled on top of me, punching and hollering. I knew I couldn't win, so I decided to just make the guy on the bottom's life as miserable as possible, digging my elbow into his eye socket and pulling on his ear with my free thumb and forefinger. The platoon eventually wrestled me off him and began to tie me to a tree with duct tape and string, laughing and gagging me with a strip of tape over my mouth. Once I had been secured to the tree, they stepped back, still laughing, telling me not to take it personally, and some began to walk back to their rucksacks. The kid whose ear I had pulled sat nursing what would be a nasty black eye, his ear bleeding in the back where I had almost succeeded in ripping it off.

I had my knife in my right pocket, and they had taped my right arm down by my side so that it was only a matter of time before I had opened the knife with my thumb and begun to cut myself free. Once I separated myself from the tree, I went after the first guys I could lay my hands on, punching and wrestling. The platoon thought this was fantastic, that I had freed myself and was now actually fighting back, even succeeding in pinning one of my sergeants on the ground and choking him with his own collar. This time, however, it only took five of them to wrestle me to the ground. I gave up once they had my neck in a vise grip and I started to feel myself pass out. But once they let go, I was at it again, wrestling with another three guys until they too defeated me.

Whenever a platoon leader or platoon sergeant joins or leaves an infantry platoon, he is likely to be assaulted in such a fashion by the men, a ceremonial rite of initiation in an all-male environment. Sergeant Montoya later told me that when he joined, it took the entire platoon to subdue him, and after they let him up, he body-slammed one of the soldiers who had attacked him into a mud puddle. Sergeant Montoya was the lead hand-to-hand combat instructor in the battalion, and no one ever messed with him after that. The men alternately called him "Yoda" or "Master Splinter" behind his back. With me it was different. The men saw that I liked to fight and wrestle but wasn't likely to do serious harm to them like

Sergeant Montoya, and they attacked me or challenged me to fights every time we went to the field. Before long, I was somehow able to fight off a few of their mass assaults, and realized that few of them considered it worth taking one of my right fists to the face in their efforts to subdue me. But most of the time, when they attacked me all together, I lost, some of them binding my arms while others tied my legs together with duct tape. In the desert, much later, after I had been defeated yet again by the Gladiator hordes after a training exercise, one of my sergeants remarked, "They must really love you, sir, because I've never seen a platoon leader get the shit kicked out of him as much as you do."

On the way out of the field the day after my first training exercise, we marched for eighteen miles in ninety-degree heat back to trucks that would take us to the barracks. Most guys in the platoon were seriously hurting by the time we made it back. They had not drank enough water while we were out in the field and had passed out by the side of the road as we marched. I walked with my new radio operator, an Asian kid from California who would later come to be called Flash, and by the time we arrived at the trucks, I was practically dragging him by the microphone tethered to his radio on a two-foot leash. The guys collapsed at the trucks, and one of them offered me the front of the truck for the ride home, telling me that was where the platoon leader usually rode. I declined, telling him he could enjoy the comfortable seat in my place, and climbed into the back with the rest of the men, who sat dusty and tired on the hard brown benches that ran along the sides. Some were removing their boots to find blisters the size of quarters, and I smiled, telling them about the blisters I had suffered in the march out of Florida Phase in Ranger School.

One of the men offered me a plug of Red Man, and though I didn't really want any tobacco at that point, only some water, I accepted it anyway, spitting out the brown juice in thick globs off the back of the truck. I was exhausted, but as I looked around at the men with me and on what we had done over the past few days, I had a tremendous feeling of satisfaction. For the first time in a year, I was enjoying my new life in the military.

VI

A STANDARD LIGHT infantry platoon in the United States Army should have thirty-four men in it: three nine-man rifle squads, two two-man machine gun teams, a radio operator, a platoon sergeant, and a lieutenant who is the platoon leader.

At 8:00 A.M. on Tuesday morning, September 11, 2001, Third Platoon, Alpha Company, 4th Battalion, 31st Infantry—my platoon—had nineteen men in the formation at Fort Drum. The Tenth Mountain Division faced a severe lack of men overall. During the past few months, my platoon had been drained from an already short size of thirty by the units headed for peacekeeping rotations in the Sinai, Bosnia, and Kosovo. As the units headed for the Balkans took what men they needed, I was left trying to figure out how to lead five-man squads in training exercises when all army tactical doctrine is formulated around nine-man squads. I was frustrated by the whole process, mainly because I knew there was some desk jockey in the Pentagon assuring the army chief of staff that the Tenth Mountain Division was at 100 percent strength.

That morning, my men and I stretched in preparation for a four-mile run. The company was scheduled for a mandatory urinalysis that day, but I had decided to do physical training beforehand. After I released three sergeants to help with the urinalysis, we were down to only sixteen men for the run.

I led the run and took it slow for the first mile, a flat straightaway along a two-lane road, to let everyone warm up. For the second mile, I picked up the pace with Sergeant Rodriguez, one of my squad leaders, to the side of the formation, yelling at the men to hold the formation as they accelerated to my pace. Sergeant Rod was a physical force. He was scheduled to be a drill sergeant in his next assignment, and I imagined that he would be a good one.

The run was two miles out and two miles back, and the turnaround point was the only sizable hill on Fort Drum, a quarter-mile steep incline that everyone called "the cut." Engineers had dynamited through heavy slate in order to connect the main buildings at Fort Drum and New York Highway 26 with this two-lane road. At the bottom was a gate that had remained open and unguarded since I had arrived at the fort. After the events of that morning, I would never see them unguarded again.

As we ran down the hill, I called out behind me, "How many fall-outs we got, Sergeant Rod?"

"Four, sir!"

"Well, men," I yelled back to the formation, "you know what we have to do."

We proceeded to run up and down the quarter-mile hill four times, one time for each of the four men who had not been able to stay in formation for the first two miles. By the time I arrived at the top on the hill for the fourth time, there were only six men left in the formation. My legs, strengthened by a full summer of cycling in the Adirondacks, including weekend trips to Lake Placid, were in better shape than many of my men's. Most of these guys spent their weekends playing video games and drinking beer. I told Sergeant Rod to wrangle up the stragglers and meet me back at the barracks. At that point I took the soldiers remaining in my formation and ran back. Setting a quick pace on the return, I had only four men beside me when we turned off the road and into the barracks to finish the run.

"When are we going to start *really* running, sir?" one of them joked.

The autumn weather had not yet arrived in upstate New York, so I remained outside and stretched in the warm sunshine while I waited for Sergeant Rod to make it back with the ten men who hadn't been able to stay in formation.

I was gulping water, trying to hydrate enough so I could piss for the urinalysis, when one of the sergeants in the company came out of the building to see me.

"Did you hear, sir? A plane crashed into the World Trade Center."

I didn't understand what he was saying. He repeated what he had said, slower and with a sense of urgency.

"Are we talking about a Cessna here, or a jumbo jet?" I asked.

"I don't know. I just heard on the radio"

71

I sat there as he walked back inside, taking another sip of water. Sergeant Rod was coming back into the barracks area now, the ten men in tow, yelling at them just as loudly as he had the first two miles.

At the moment, though, I was thinking about the plane.

There are a thousand ways to use the word "fuck" in the English language, and in the army, you learn all of them. In this case I muttered the word aloud, speaking to myself, surprised but not yet alarmed. At this point, I had a mental image of a small plane leaving a scar on the side of the World Trade Center but little else.

Still, I was worried. One of my best friends from high school in East Tennessee, Ben Patch, lived about two blocks away from the World Trade Center, in Battery Park City.

A few minutes later, one of the married soldiers who had been home for breakfast came in from the parking lot.

"I just heard on the radio that two planes crashed in the World Trade Center."

"No," I corrected him, "just one."

"No, sir! Another one just hit it."

"Shut the fuck up."

"I'm serious, sir!"

I headed into my office and logged on to the Internet to try to figure out what was going on. CNN's Web site was overwhelmed, as was the *New York Times* site. I couldn't even get my e-mail.

I headed upstairs and came upon a group of soldiers huddled around the television outside the laundry room. They told me one of the towers had fallen.

How can the freaking tower fall? I asked myself.

And then I saw it—the video—the jet banking hard and plunging into the tower. The fireball erupting from both sides and the smoke rising.

"Damn."

"Yeah. That was the second plane."

"Fuck."

We stood motionless and silent, glued to the screen. And then we saw the second tower begin to collapse.

"There it goes," someone whispered.

And there it went. The top began to crumble onto the rest of the tower, and all of us hoped against hope that somehow the collapse would arrest itself, that it would somehow stop in a freeze frame.

Within minutes someone told me that a plane had hit the Pentagon as well. I believed them immediately, because after what I had just seen, anything seemed possible. But one of my sergeants was incredulous.

"No fucking way," he said. "The Pentagon is too well guarded."

But he was wrong, and we soon saw the images from Washington. There was the familiar shape of the Pentagon, now with furious thick smoke billowing at one end.

"Well, I guess we're all getting promoted," someone tried to joke.

Nobody laughed.

The room was silent for a long time. By now about twenty of us were huddled around the small television. Each of us could have watched this alone in his room or office, but I think we all felt a need to see this with one another, if only to be assured that it was actually happening. That this was real.

I was the first one to speak.

"Better pack your bags, boys."

BY NOON ALL of our company had packed our equipment and were ready to deploy to New York City to help with disaster relief. The fact that we had just that morning been relieved from being the "immediate readiness company" for the division helped to expedite our preparation. All companies in the Tenth Mountain Division take a thirty-day turn as the IRC, ready to deploy within twenty-four hours in the event of an emergency. As such, most of our gear was still packed and ready to go.

Before long we got the alert for preparation to deploy. Captain Rogers had received orders and came down to the company to brief us. All the platoon leaders were told the classified location in the New York City area where we were being sent. There were worries the attacks could provoke rioting and civil unrest in Manhattan. Captain Rogers was, as always, a ball of energy. Several times in the next few days, we would need to go for a run together in the afternoon to relieve the tension.

My men were ready and willing to go. In the immediate aftermath of 9/11, I think all Americans were ready to do whatever was needed to help defend their country.

I stayed at the office late that night. Everyone stayed late, actually, not wanting to leave work, not sure when we would all get on buses or helicopters for the ride south to the city. I tried to keep everyone's spirits high with an impromptu rendition of the Beastie Boys' "No Sleep 'Til Brooklyn."

That night, as I drove home to my apartment, I called my mother. She had been trying all day to reach me but had not been able to get through. I had been in my office, where my cell phone did not get service.

I told my mother we were preparing to deploy to New York City, and that I was excited by the prospect. I knew that all my friends around the country—especially those in New York—were feeling helpless now, and I felt I was one of the few people who could do something about the events of the day.

My mother quickly tempered my excitement.

"I don't want you to have to sort through those bodies," she said, and then broke down crying.

I had never heard my mother like this. Usually when I heard her cry it was because of something I had done. In high school, whenever I was particularly unruly, she would sob about how my behavior reflected on what a poor mother she was. Looking back on it, we both found it comical. This was different. That night, I listened to a new tone in her voice, scared and anxious, but mostly sad. That night my mother wept for her son's innocence.

Until that day, she had still seen me as a curly-haired eight-year-old boy and had not come to grips with what I did for a living. All my life as a soldier beforehand had just been dressing up and playing army in the woods to her—essentially the same thing I had done as a kid. But the events of September 11, 2001, changed the way lots of people looked at things, and my mother was no exception.

I calmed my mother down, and talked about the stoic Spartan and Confederate women who watched their sons and husbands march off to war with their emotions tightly guarded.

It may sound absurd, but such historical arguments resonate with my mother, as they do with all Southerners, and she immediately composed herself as a Greek mother might have before her son marched off to Thermopylae over two thousand years ago. We both knew that in the days after September 11, with a son in such a position as I was, people back home would instinctively look to my mother for her reactions. If she remained calm and strong, so would they. If she became hysterical, they might be tempted to as well.

After I said good-bye, I called several other people. I called all my friends in New York City to make sure they were safe. Luckily they were. The Port Authority had evacuated my high school buddy Patch across the Hudson to New Jersey, and though he didn't know it at the time, he would not be allowed to return to his apartment for several weeks.

When I got home I wrote out two checks. One was to my landlord for two months of rent. The other was to the lady who lived in the other half of the rental house who had promised to look after my apartment and the whitewater kayaks I had stowed under the stairs. I told her to use the money I gave her if the house needed anything while I was gone.

THE NEXT DAY, we all arrived at work early, excited about leaving for New York City. But that afternoon we were ordered to stand down because the National Guard would do the task we had initially been given.

That night I left work frustrated. I had joined the army looking to make a difference, to have a direct impact on things while still young. I knew that most of my classmates from college would be toiling away at law school or on Wall Street while I might be keeping the peace in Kosovo or Bosnia. Now it looked more and more like we would get passed over.

But within days another mission sprung up. We were going somewhere after all, and this looked to be a mission out of the country. And we were excited again.

Those weeks we spent at Drum after we were alerted and before we left were good ones, which is ironic considering how the rest of the country was in turmoil, grappling with the most devastating peacetime attack in U.S. history. We couldn't go far from post since we had to make a two-hour recall formation, and we bonded during those weeks as only men with a common mission can. To the civilian populace, gearing up for a war entails soul-searching and constant worrying, but for soldiers an excitement fills the air, an anticipation of things to come. We got all the time and ammunition to train that we wanted, as opposed to the tightly rationed allotments we were used to. I remember wrestling with my men outside at the rifle range, fighting them off five at a time with wild punches and kicks, just to relieve tension. I remember getting our weapons ready, firing every day. I remember building airplane pallets full of MREs, bottled water, and duffel bags.

I also remember the talks I had with my men during those weeks. We talked about everything. We talked about the prospect of war, of leaving girlfriends and wives behind, of catching Osama bin Laden. I had a picture of him in my office cut out from the *New York Post*, and my men would argue about which one of us would be the first to put a bullet between his eyes.

I remember watching all the constant media coverage at first, but after a while, I just tuned it out. I didn't watch any of the President's speeches to the nation; instead I read and spent time alone. I didn't own a television, so it was easier to avoid the media orgy. I do remember being scared by some of the rhetoric, though, such as conservative columnist Ann Coulter's remark that the prudent thing to do would be invade all Muslim countries and convert them to Christianity. In that environment, I felt genuinely sorry for the Indian people who operated the Dunkin' Donuts on my way to work. I think they were Hindu, not Muslim, but I knew such subtle differences wouldn't matter to an angry populace.

Because the company had so few men, Captain Rogers reorganized it to make two full platoons. Second Platoon ceased to exist as we cannibalized it to bulk up my platoon, Third Platoon, as well as First Platoon. A budding rivalry had existed between us and First Platoon, one that would intensify now that we were the only two platoons in the company. I didn't care much for their platoon leader and Sergeant Montoya's style differed wildly from their platoon sergeant's, a bear of a man the men called "Big Daddy." I liked Big Daddy well enough—he always took the time out of his schedule to offer advice and became a sort of father figure to a lot of the men in the company, myself included—but my squad leaders did not care for him.

As part of the dissolution of Second Platoon, I got a new squad leader we all grew to call Ray, his first name, even though he was a staff sergeant. At first we called him his first name as a joke and later as a nod to his laid-back style around

Sergeant Montoya and me. It was more like we were old friends as opposed to soldiers within a rigid rank structure. With his men, he was different—intense and relentless about training. He was twenty-nine years old and got along well with my other sergeants. But more than the other sergeants, he took the time to mentor me one-on-one in some of the little things.

Whereas the higher-ranking platoon sergeants of the company helped me to become a better leader, Ray helped me to become a better soldier. I was a good marksman, but Ray had initially trained as a sniper and made me a lot better at shooting by showing me how to acquire targets faster and engage them at longer distances than I had learned to. He helped our platoon come up with new standard operating procedures (SOPs) for markings and signals. We used special markings in the field to identify things like cleared bunkers and rooms, while visual signals helped me to communicate with my squad leaders when the radios failed or when the noise of battle would make it hard to hear. Ray showed me other tricks, like how to staunch the bleeding from a bullet wound with a tampon. Field dressings were expensive and scarce, the reasoning went, but tampons could be cheaply bought in any drugstore.

I was grateful to have Ray as part of my team, and we became fast friends as we spent more time together over the coming months. We shared a common sense of humor, and by the time we would see combat, we shared a kind of battlefield telepathy. He knew what I wanted before I asked for it, and I knew exactly how to use his squad in tough situations.

The other squad leaders joked and griped that Ray's squad got all the tough missions, but I couldn't help the fact that I always felt most at ease with him in charge.

We spent the days before we left packing and repacking. We were given a detailed list of necessary items that included our new desert fatigues as well as "civilian clothes," which we all thought was strange. It made sense to bring a set of civilian clothes on peacetime deployments, especially those in the United States where you might travel off post. But this was war. How were we supposed to dress for that? If the shit hit the fan, did I want to be caught wearing Armani or Wal-Mart? In the end I threw a pair of blue jeans into the bag with a flannel shirt.

On the third of October, with our bags finally packed and deployment orders signed by the Pentagon, we loaded onto the chartered Delta Airlines jet that was to take us to our new station. We learned we would initially be deploying to Kuwait and Qatar but would be given secret intelligence briefings on Afghanistan. We had no idea what our mission would be, but we were ready for anything.

We were the first conventional unit to deploy as part of Operation Enduring Freedom, so the crew of the airliner treated us in high style. All the senior sergeants and officers flew in first class, where we had our own televisions and leather recliners. The flight attendants decorated the plane with patriotic banners and cards, and the pilots let some of the guys take turns in the cockpit. It seemed an absurd way to be going to war.

I dozed off about eight hours into the flight, and when I awakened, I looked out the window to see nothing but light browns and blues. I had never seen a desert before, and as the plane banked left and descended into Kuwait International Airport, I stared down into the vast expanse of sand in awe. I began to feel I would get to know the desert awfully well before the War on Terror was over.

VII

Upon landing, we boarded buses and drove off into the Kuwait desert, away from the city and along one of the highways that ring the urban areas of the country. After thirty minutes, we arrived at a walled compound called Camp Doha, guarded by civilian employees with assault rifles and blue Kevlar helmets. We drove through the gates and down the brown road leading to what would be our home for the next five months.

They quartered us in a warehouse on the base about the size of a football field and portioned into sections to accommodate all the transient personnel who came in and out. We got two sections in which to house our entire company, making for cramped but not uncomfortable living conditions. We were initially just happy to get out of the heat. Although it was already October, the temperature in Kuwait was still in the nineties. The military policemen who escorted us on the way in pointed to the armed guards at the gate and noted that in August—when daily temperatures could reach 120 degrees— the guards' shirts soaked completely through and some guards would pass out on duty from the oppressive heat.

The latrines were fifty meters down the road from the warehouse, located in elevated trailers. They had real toilets and a limited supply of hot water. And although they were disgusting and littered with graffiti and scum and pubic hair and often six inches of standing water, they were a hell of a lot better than we had expected, so no one complained. Quite frankly, we had thought we'd be living in tents in the desert, so these accommodations were actually welcoming.

Camp Doha was a small base located at the tip of the western peninsula, on the outskirts of Kuwait City. To the north, east, and west was the Persian Gulf, and a solitary road to the south led to the highways circling the city. The camp perimeter was about five miles around. I know this because we used to run around it for morning physical training and would hike around it three times in the dead of night with our rucksacks on to keep our feet "hard" and our bodies used to marching long distances. Those brutal midnight walks around Camp Doha haunt me to this day, as my radioman and I would walk together and often compete to see who had the biggest blisters by the end.

Within a small perimeter, Camp Doha featured a surprising number of amenities. There was a PX, a barbershop, and a movie theater that played movies that had just recently completed their runs in America. There was also a massive gym, financed by the Kuwaiti royal family, which rivaled any fitness center in America and which featured a hardwood basketball court, a boxing ring, a volleyball court, aerobics rooms, a weight room, and a cardio-fitness room. The gym was the social center of the base, and I often went there two or three times a day. Over the next three months, the company XO and I would hit the weights hard six times a week, packing dense muscle onto our frames and gaining weight from all the food we ate at the chow hall. By the time I left, I would be close to the same weight and level of fitness I had achieved just before reporting to Ranger School.

Our unit's mission was unclear from the start. In fact, we spent the first few days wondering why U.S. Army Central Command had requested us in the first place. But eventually the folks at Doha decided that we could augment the convoy escort missions currently taking place all over Kuwait. To do this, we had to sign for vehicles, Humvees, which very few soldiers in our unit had ever operated before. We were a light infantry company, which meant that we normally only had one vehicle in our entire company. Our platoon was used to walking everywhere we went or being ferried over long distances by helicopter or on trucks. Few of the soldiers were licensed to drive military vehicles, and only the guys who had been in mechanized units prior to their time in the Tenth knew how to conduct regular maintenance on Humvees. Nonetheless, I would sign for eight pristine, mostly new Humvees that I would then sign over to my soldiers. All the Humvees were in far better condition than the Humvees we had at Fort Drum, which were almost twenty years old and broke down as often as they ran. The vehicles at Camp Doha were part of the cache of vehicles, tanks, helicopters, and Bradley fighting vehicles the army had kept in storage in the Middle East in the event of contingency operations against Iraq. (In October 2001, the eventual war with Iraq was still some sixteen months away.) In addition to the vehicles, the army hired Kuwaiti mechanics to maintain all the equipment, which they did as well as any mechanic back home, if not better.

Probably because the Humvees were such a novelty for my guys, they immediately began painting slogans and names on them as soon as I divided the platoon into four-man teams and assigned each team a vehicle. Our Humvees had names ranging from the obscene ("The Shocker") to the animal ("The Jackal"). Our vehicle was christened by myself and my forward observer, who hailed from the same section of the country that I did—just over the Georgia state line from Chattanooga. We named our Humvee "The General Lee," after the car in *The Dukes of Hazzard*, and gave ourselves "call signs" in keeping with the show. The forward observer from Georgia was hereafter solely known as Uncle Jesse, his radioman as Cooter, my radioman as Flash, and I was Luke Duke.

On my orders, the guys in my platoon got their hands on some spray paint and stenciled GENERAL LEE above both doors and with thick black duct tape numbered an "01" on both doors. After much internal debate, however, we decided to paint an American flag on the roof in lieu of the original General Lee's Confederate battle flag. Not that anyone on the Kuwaiti highways would have noticed the difference. As such, the General Lee was ostentatious enough.

For the next several months, I spent most of my time leading convoys throughout the Kuwaiti desert and into the cities. It was boring and tedious. I would often catch Flash falling asleep at the wheel, and I always felt sorry for whomever—usually Cooter—sat in the turret with the mounted machine gun in the dust and heat. Sometimes, our missions would last for more than twelve hours, the record being a thirty-six-hour marathon down at the Kuwaiti port, securing a giant boat and escorting more than 130 vehicles back to Camp Doha. On especially long missions, I would either take turns driving or sit in the turret to give Cooter a rest. Mostly, I sat in the passenger seat, talking on one radio with Captain Rogers back at Doha and on my other radio with the rest of the Humvees in the convoy.

The long and boring missions would not have been half as interesting were it not for the ever-precarious physical condition of "The General," without a doubt the shittiest Humvee in all of Kuwait. Traveling through a busy intersection one Friday morning, the General decided to lose its left rear door, which flew off and went tumbling down the street. While we held up the honking, impatient Kuwaiti traffic in all four directions, Uncle Jesse and I cursed and tied the door back on with duct tape and nylon parachute cord. On another mission, the engine died and the General had to be towed back to the garage, where it stayed for a month while the Kuwaiti mechanics worked on it. During that month, passersby at Camp Doha—both my own soldiers and also men I had never seen before—would stop me on the street and ask me how the General was. By that point the General Lee had amassed quite a following of admirers, and it was a treat when Uncle Jesse and I spotted it being test driven around Doha one day by a small Kuwaiti mechanic, a sure sign that our Humvee was almost ready to go again.

Unfortunately, when we got the General Lee back, its engine still wasn't very strong. But it jumped well, as we found whenever we took it out into the desert and tackled the sand dunes. Every time we lifted off, we made sure to give a good "Yee-Haw!" as we rose into the air.

On those long missions, we all got to know each other better and delighted in ribbing one another and telling stories—both fact and fiction—about the others in the Humvee. Most of the abuse was reserved for Flash, a shy, quiet kid who had the misfortune of being from San Francisco and was therefore always being kidded about being from the "San Francisco 'Gay' Area." He was also the only Asian guy in the platoon, the son of two Chinese immigrants who emigrated from Vietnam after his father fought for five years alongside American forces in the ARVN. So in addition to being teased as an accused homosexual, Flash also had to endure all the good-natured racial stereotypes hurled forth with aplomb by Uncle Jesse.

Flash almost never said anything in response, being the junior man in the Humvee and only a private. He just sat there smiling, his face getting redder and redder with every insult from Uncle Jesse. The only time he ever spoke up was when Uncle Jesse would make a crack about Flash being from Vietnam, at which point Flash would counter that being from Vietnam was infinitely preferable to being an ignorant rube from North Georgia like Uncle Jesse. Cooter would sit in the turret during these insult sessions laughing at his good fortune that Uncle Jesse had not yet begun to similarly insult him. But Cooter wasn't any more exempt than I was, though I could be just as acidic as anyone else and countered Uncle Jesse's comic insults with my own offerings.

I had liked Flash from the start. He was eighteen and hadn't known a thing about the radio he was given at Fort Drum until I taught him what little I knew and then sent him down to the company radio operators to try and learn something more from them. We had done a few exercises together before we left for Kuwait, and every month we sat down to do an evaluation of what he had done both wrong and right in the month previous and make a list of things for him to work on. He was a quick learner and, despite his lack of experience, rarely made the same mistake twice. After I chided him for not having enough batteries during one field problem, the next time he came with enough for twice the duration of the field exercise we were on.

He also learned that the unspoken duty of the radio operator was not only to work the radios but also to look after the platoon leader and make sure I wasn't forgetting anything. It paid to have experience and intelligence as a radio operator, and while Flash needed more of the former, he had plenty of the latter. Before missions, we would meet in the barracks to check each other over. He ran through a list of things, making sure I had everything, and I did the same for him. After a few months, I would walk up to the Company Operations Center to make final preparations, and by the time I came back, Flash had already loaded my gear into the Humvee, ready to go.

I went out of the way to explain things to Flash, things that didn't have anything to do with his job but things that would make Flash a better soldier. I taught him tactical operations orders and small unit tactics while we rode around in convoys. On small missions, where the full complement of the mighty General Lee was not needed, we would travel—just the two of us—in a Jeep Cherokee, listening to the awful Kuwaiti radio stations and making fun of the song selection. On long rides in the desert, he would keep us both awake by asking lots of questions about both of our jobs, the missions, and all the stuff going on in the world, which was plenty. When we had run through all those topics, we would then talk about home. I asked more questions than he did, about his family and his high school, keeping in mind that he had graduated just a few months earlier.

Uncle Jesse had grown up only about forty miles from me, in the mountains north of Atlanta. He thought about going to college, but he and his wife had their first child at a young age. So after high school, he joined the army and had been stationed in Germany—where he and his wife had their second child—before coming to Fort Drum. We were exactly the same age, having graduated from high school the same year just a few miles down Interstate 75 from each other. But it struck me how different our lives had become since high school graduation.

Still, there were more similarities between the two of us than there were differences. Uncle Jesse knew that despite my education and higher station within the army, I was essentially the same as him, the product of the same Appalachian environment and upbringing. There was no fooling him with my fancy vocabulary and officer's rank. We shared a common vernacular, and others in the platoon noticed how my accent became more pronounced whenever I told stories and laughed with Uncle Jesse. Uncle Jesse was already balding and might have seemed ten years older than he was if it weren't for his boundless energy and never-ending wisecracks, delivered in a familiar, heavy north Georgia twang that reminded me of home.

His radio operator, Cooter, was from upstate New York, near West Point, and had briefly been stationed in the 101st Airborne before coming to Fort Drum. Cooter was about twenty-one, quick to laugh at Uncle Jesse and me, and affable enough until he had sat in the turret harness for more than ten hours. He was always sidling up to either Uncle Jesse or me, cracking jokes, waiting for us to begin harassing one of the other soldiers for his amusement.

It wasn't too bad a life, but that was the problem. We were largely unchallenged by the daily ennui of Camp Doha and Kuwait. We had expected combat, and instead we got the highway patrol. After six weeks of guarding uneventful convoys, spending hours upon hours at the airport waiting on flights of servicemen to come into the country, and living in a drab warehouse, we began to get bored.

Boredom, in the army, is the fertile field in which the seeds of mischief are sown. In the barracks, for example, woe unto the man who leaves his camera unattended on top of his bed. Our SOP for this contingency was for us to pass the camera around the barracks until either every man had stuffed the camera down his pants to photograph his genitals or the camera ran out of film. Many a soldier walked back from the old Kuwaiti man who processed film at the PX with an embarrassed, angry look on his face and a pocket full of photographs of other men's penises.

At night, my machine gun teams would take their mattresses off their beds, wrapping them around themselves and taping them with heavy layers of duct tape to keep the mattresses up and around their bodies. Then they would step out into the street, where—to the amusement of onlookers—they would proceed to sumo wrestle on the pavement. Inside the barracks, you might see a group of soldiers huddled around the television on any given night, watching movies sent from home, and another group of soldiers creeping around the bunks with pellet guns, shooting one another and any "civilians on the battlefield," as soldiers asleep on their bunks were known.

One of the new soldiers in the gun teams, Gregory, a tiny private straight out of high school who couldn't have weighed more than 110 pounds, kept himself busy by ambushing me once a day in the barracks, jumping on my back and trying to wrestle me to the ground or choke me. The platoon always looked forward to our fights, as I weighed twice as much and always kicked his ass, once flipping him over my head so hard I was afraid I had broken his back. He just laughed, though, relishing his role as the underdog and fan favorite.

Gregory's size and fighting spirit were typical of my machine gunners. He served as the assistant gunner to another one of my crazier soldiers, Junk, named for the way his Romanian name sounded when pronounced by American accents. In a two-man gun team, one man carries the heavy machine gun, the M-240B, while the other carries the tripod and extra belt-fed, 7.62mm ammunition. The machine gunners and assistant gunners had two of the toughest jobs in the platoon because of the enormous weight they were required to carry while being responsible for the majority of the platoon's firepower. In other units, the machine gun, its ammunition, and its tripod were split up between three men. But some genius in the Pentagon had decided that the Tenth Mountain would make do with two-man teams. In a further ironic and cruel twist, both of my machine gun teams were comprised of some of the smallest guys in the platoon. All the same, they were wickedly fit and tremendously competent. Junk had won the battalion's "Best Machine Gunner" competition almost a year earlier, and he had only gotten better since. The other machine gunner, McCauley, wasn't too far behind him, deadly in his own right.

"Crazy" Carl McCauley is one of those interesting characters you can only find in the U.S. Army. Raised in Idaho, he had joined the army at the age of seventeen and, like Junk, had yet to grow up. He was rambunctious and wild and gave my sergeants a tough time. Along with his crazy stories and the lies he invented, he was phenomenally undisciplined. But he had taken an early liking to me and looked up to me as a big brother. I climbed and hiked and knew all about the outdoor stuff he himself liked to do.

Junk and McCauley made me laugh with their antics, and I knew something about them that made them worth keeping around: they were born trigger-pullers. These men, I felt sure, would never hesitate to kill the enemy. Our general society may have trouble dealing with such man-boys, but in combat, they are priceless. I couldn't get enough of them. The gunners were tremendously proud of their jobs and had an esprit de corps the rest of the platoon both admired and resented. The platoon laughed at all the gun teams' antics, but my squad leaders and other sergeants grumbled that the gunners lacked discipline and responsibility. I couldn't deny that. In many ways, the machine gunners were the embodiment of boys in men's clothing. They had the maturity of sixteen-year-olds but were trusted enough to carry the strength of the platoon in their arms.

Mostly the soldiers sought out ways to spend their vast reserves of unused testosterone during our downtime in Kuwait, either by lifting weights in the gym or sitting in the latrine or port-a-potties outside the barracks to beat off to the contraband porno magazines they had accumulated. *Playboy* was tame compared to the filth some guys had hidden underneath their mattresses. Our artillery soldiers who served as forward observers, like Uncle Jesse and Cooter, were more open with their pornography. Known as the Fire Support Team—or "FIST"—they had pictures of women on their walls in sexual situations consistent with their team's acronym. Others had pictures of nude women pasted onto the opposite side of the laminated maps of Kuwait they used on missions.

I seemed to spend most of my time at the airport, too tired or busy to consider women or their skewed pornographic representations. Planes inbound for Kuwait were notoriously unreliable and often kept us waiting for hours at a time. I envied the soldiers lined up to leave the country and laughed at the groups of nervous servicemen who trod off the planes coming into the country.

We had been disappointed by our experience in Kuwait thus far. We left the United States in the aftermath of 9/11 expecting to kill bad guys and exact revenge for the attacks on the Trade Center and the Pentagon. Instead, my guys had taken to wryly describing our mission in Kuwait as "Operation Enduring Boredom."

Most servicemen, it should be said, are not "trigger-pullers." For every man who pulls a trigger in combat, seven men and women exist to fill supporting roles behind him. The soldiers on the planes that arrived in Kuwait were mostly the mechanics, military policemen, computer programmers, cooks, supply sergeants, and others who inhabited Camp Doha on a year-round basis. They had likely been told by their former superiors in the United States they were entering a real, no-shit war zone in the Middle East and had to be prepared for the *absolute worst*—advice that was completely ridiculous given the placid reality on the ground in Kuwait. True, some of the young Arab men in the small towns outside Kuwait City gave us ugly looks now and then as we drove through. But most Kuwaitis went out of their way to be friendly. Their children leaned out the windows of their parents' black Mercedes to wave at us, their toothy smiles spread across their faces in cartoon grins. Arab kids are just like American kids, awkward and funny, and my soldiers and I usually responded to the kids by sticking our tongues out or making funny faces in return.

The Kuwaitis we encountered on the street were mostly friendly. They only became angry when our soldiers hit on the young Kuwaiti women in the shopping mall, like normal nineteen-year-old American boys usually do. That was over the line in the eyes of the watchful Arab males. But in restaurants and coffeehouses, they met us with smiles and nods of the head when we had expected scowls and insults in the aftermath of September 11. That sentiment did not change until months later, after we had left and the military buildup against Iraq began. That was when the growing anti-American sentiment resulting from the impending invasion of Iraq led to the shootings of personnel in Kuwait.

Despite the safety of Kuwait at the time, when our charges first got off the aircraft and onto the bus, they were usually pretty nervous—expecting, I guess, bomb-toting terrorists to jump out from behind every bush on the way from the airport to Camp Doha. America had been living in a state of constant fear in the months after September 11, waiting for the next terrorist attack. Soldiers recently assigned to the Middle East were doubly nervous. While those who had lived in Kuwait for a few months carried themselves with confidence and an understanding of how secure the country really was, the "fresh meat" coming into the country was initially scared to death. Normally, I would get onto the bus first, all smiles, introduce myself, and assure them they would all be okay on their way to Camp Doha. After I got off the bus, I would laugh with Ray at the wide-eyed looks of terror on the faces of the new arrivals upon seeing a lieutenant from the Tenth Mountain Division laden with body armor and loaded weaponry welcoming them into the country.

The idea for Operational Plan C—which we referred to as "OpPlan Charlie"—arose out of a discussion between Ray and me as we waited for a planeful of colonels flying into the country. How funny would it be, we asked, if we treated the people coming into Kuwait as if they really were entering a full-blown combat zone? OpPlan Charlie was the result of those laughs Ray and I shared at the airport. Eventually we got the whole platoon in on it.

Late one night, around two-thirty in the morning, we left the airport with approximately twenty new arrivals loaded into a charter bus. We had four Humvees with us, two of which traveled in the front and two of which traveled in the rear. Ray's truck led the way while I played "sheepdog" with the General Lee in the rear, rounding up any stragglers and making sure no one took a wrong turn. It was amazing how often one of the buses would fail to follow the others and head off in the wrong direction. All four Humvees had machine guns mounted on the top, as much to reassure the people being escorted of their safety as to dissuade potential terrorist attacks. In reality, four or forty or even four hundred gun trucks would have been little help in the event of a sniper or single determined terrorist armed with an RPG by the highway. But the soldiers on the bus didn't know that, and we didn't think much of it either since we all knew we were being used as part of what the army calls a "show of force" mission.

I had developed the practice of placing one of my soldiers on the bus along with a radio for these trips between Camp Doha and the airport. That way, the soldier could relay any messages I had for the driver and get the driver back on course should he make a wrong turn.

The soldier I put on the bus that night was Cooter, and we had given him specific instructions. Upon boarding the bus, Cooter was to read aloud from the "Camp Doha Threat Siren Card" we had all been given upon arrival in Kuwait. In the event of an attack, the way things worked at Doha was a siren

97

would sound. A high-pitched wailing siren meant a SCUD attack. A beeping siren meant a chemical attack. A continuous siren meant a general attack in which everyone on post was supposed to kit up in full gear and prepare for assault. It sounds more serious than it was at the time. Until GPWD II ("Great Patriotic War in the Desert, Part II," aka "Operation Iraqi Freedom"), the siren system had not yet been used in a real-world scenario.

After Cooter read the card, the folks on the bus were even more nervous than they had been when they first got on. So Cooter decided to improvise a little bit and told all the people on the bus to keep their faces away from the windows and to keep the shades down so as not to offer any would-be snipers easy targets. As we rolled out of the airport, Ray got on the radio and told Cooter to make the truck driver keep it close. "We don't want what happened last time," Ray ominously warned. Cooter's volume knob on his radio was kept all the way up so everyone on the bus in addition to Cooter could hear what Ray was saying.

They immediately asked Cooter what happened last time.

"Terrorist attack," Cooter deadpanned. "It was bad. We lost a few people. Good men too. Good, good men. Damn shame."

The soldiers in the bus sat back stunned and scared out of their wits. Not half as scared as they were, however, when Ray screamed over the radio, "Cooter! Get their heads down! We're picking up something ahead on thermals."

Cooter instructed the soldiers on the bus—who had no idea we didn't even have thermal sights to begin with—to get ready to assume the crash position. He then yelled some

Arabic-sounding gibberish to the driver, who looked back, now confused and scared in his own right.

Finally I got on the radio: "This is Gladiator Six! We have a confirmed target up ahead. Initiate OpPlan Charlie!"

The Humvees screeched into action on the otherwise deserted four-lane highway. Two gun trucks moved over to the side of the bus and pointed their machine guns out toward the desert, while Cooter swung into high gear on the bus, yelling, "Everybody down on the ground! Hug the floor!"

Cooter pointed his M4 carbine at the terrified Kuwaiti bus driver and shouted, "Keep this bus fucking moving, old man! Don't stop for anything!"

The soldiers on the bus, cowering on the floor, were in tears or trying their best to be brave. Cooter later reported that one soldier had cried out, "Oh God, I don't want to die!"

We rode the whole way back to Camp Doha like that, with the soldiers on the floor of the bus. We dropped them off, shell-shocked and trembling, at their barracks before going to breakfast. We hadn't slept in twenty-four hours, but the adventures of OpPlan Charlie gave us all plenty to talk and laugh about around the table. It had been a cruel joke, and we had certainly gone over the line, but that's what happens when you give infantrymen a bullshit mission and bore them to death for weeks. Afterward, Ray and I felt sure the soldiers would report us and cause us to lose our jobs, but they never did. I guess they were too embarrassed when they learned they had been the targets of our prank.

VIII

DESPITE THE OPPRESSIVE boredom, a few good things came out of our Kuwait experience. The best thing was the amount of training we were able to accomplish. My platoon shot live bullets from their weapons every week. While that may not sound like much of an accomplishment, anyone who has served more than a day in the army knows that's an impressive feat of logistics. Back in the U.S., a trip to the firing range was an "emotional experience" that had to be planned weeks in advance. The paperwork you had to submit just to fire your weapon on a rifle range was so intimidating that some officers just gave up and stopped trying. And you rarely had as much ammunition as you'd requested. In Kuwait, we simply drew some ammunition from the ASP (Ammo Supply Point), drove out into the desert, and shot at targets we put up ourselves with no one around to look over our backs at our training.

Captain Rogers was the engine that drove the company, keeping us busy with a relentless training schedule. He knew the longer we stayed in the barracks, the more bored we would get, the crazier we would get, and the more trouble we would get into. He had caught wind of the OpPlan Charlie antics that made my platoon the heroes of the company and resolved to keep us even busier so we wouldn't have time for such pranks again. Captain Rogers also knew that if we were to see combat, we might save lives because we'd had tough prior training. A pound of sweat in training is worth an ounce of blood in combat, the saying went. Plus, Captain Rogers hated the confines of Camp Doha, where he had little to do aside from think about the fact that he was expecting his first child back home in New York, a child he knew he would not see born. So he dragged us to the rifle ranges out in the desert all days of the week and trained with us there to keep his mind on the military side of things. We had a new executive officer, my friend Bobby whom I had replaced as platoon leader, and Captain Rogers kept Bobby busy day and night getting us ammunition and land to train on.

On account of Captain Rogers' well-intentioned harrassment, Bobby was the most tortured member of the company, and we all did our part to tease him, even the enlisted soldiers. They had a thousand different names for him. "Bobby Doha!" they would scream out to him across the post as he trod off to his cramped office.

One day, as Bobby wrestled with the barrel-chested first sergeant (or, more accurately, got his ass kicked), my eagle-eyed soldiers spied that Bobby was wearing white athletic socks with his desert boots, a violation of uniform. From that day on, Bobby was known solely as "Bobby Whitesocks." He is a great officer and was respected and well-liked by the men. I have no doubt that he can be anything he wants to be in the military, general included.

In addition to the shooting on the marksmanship ranges, we also trained in areas that simulated the types of objectives we could see in Afghanistan or Iraq. In one exercise, I built a "terrorist training camp" in the middle of the desert, out of an old tent, some concertina wire, and a few old oil drums, and then had my men raid the objective at night. I placed targets all around the tent to simulate terrorists or Taliban fighters, and my men shot the targets while securing the camp. On another exercise, we set up targets in an abandoned women's prison just outside of Camp Doha and practiced moving through the crumbling urban terrain, clearing rooms, using our infrared lasers to acquire targets at night, and treating and evacuating simulated casualties. We also conducted a similar operation at an abandoned satellite dish compound.

Back at Doha, when the ASP was depleted, we begged, borrowed, and outright stole ammunition to train with. The Special Forces teams stationed with us gave us what they didn't want—machine gun ammunition, plastic explosives—in exchange for what we had in surplus that they needed, like M4 carbine ammunition. Ray had a connection over in USAEUR (United States Army Europe) who sent us another hundred thousand rounds of ammunition. And when all else failed, I had McCauley dive down at night into the amnesty boxes—locations where soldiers can drop unauthorized ammunition without fear of reprisal—and put his hands on whatever he could find there. Unlike in America, where we kept all the ammunition in a central, guarded location that made it secure but tough to get to in a hurry, in Kuwait we often kept ammunition under our cots if we had a mission that night or the next day.

Along with the shooting and exercises in the desert, we continued to keep up our physical training by lifting weights and running around the camp's perimeter. We also continued to march at least fifteen miles once a month, though the hard sandy pavement tore up our feet. Flash helped me pull off my boots after one long march, and we discovered large blisters oozing blood on the soles of my feet. Flash laughed at me for not having tougher feet and took pictures of my blisters to keep for posterity before helping me drain them with a syringe.

While we trained, we continued our missions and mischief. On one mission to secure a port to allow a Marine Expeditionary Unit (MEU) to leave the country, we ran riot among the dry-docked boats, fooling around when it became apparent the port was secured already. We took a picture of me dressed up as an al-Qaeda terrorist, climbing out of a boat while Ray pointed his weapon at me like I had just been captured. We also ended up liberating a hundred-pound boat propeller and taking it back to Doha. When we found we couldn't ship it back to the States, we drove it out deep into the desert, wrote our names on it, and stuck it in the middle of a crossroads. I can only imagine what the locals thought when they drove by that propeller planted in the desert of northwest Kuwait.

When we weren't on missions, the sergeants tried to keep

the soldiers as busy as they could with additional physical training in the gym or on the dirt track. We also organized trips into Kuwait City. My guys loved visiting American restaurants near the beach, like Applebee's and Chili's. Their only disappointment was that the restaurants didn't serve any real beer. All they had was the nonalcoholic variety, which tastes a lot like fizzy brown apple juice. We drank a lot of it, anyway, hoping against hope that if we drank enough we might feel a buzz.

We organized other healthy ways to release all our surplus testosterone. I captained our company soccer team, which went undefeated in the Kuwaiti Inter-base Soccer League. Every Friday night, we played against a different team from Doha or one of the air force bases nearby. We played on a dirt playing field, and playing along the back line, I always had nasty cuts and scrapes on my legs from all the slide tackles I made on the rough surface. I didn't have the skill some of the other players did, but I punished anyone who drifted too close to our goal. I felt sorry for the teams we played against. They weren't prepared for how physical our team was. Our guys had so much pent-up energy they simply beat the other teams into submission.

The strain of being away from home for so long and not having many things to do, however, continued to take its toll. The men got cranky and often mouthed off to other units stationed in our barracks. This wasn't a problem until they picked a fight with the Navy SEALs who lived on the other side of the wall that partitioned the warehouse where we were quartered.

It happened during the 2001 World Series. The Yankees

were playing the Diamondbacks, and since so many guys in the Tenth Mountain Division were from New York, we had a lot of Yankees fans who woke up at three in the morning to watch the games live. We also had a rather large anti-Yankee contingent who also got up, to jeer them. As a lifelong Red Sox fan, I found myself enthusiastically cheering for Arizona.

The SEALs began to complain about our noise in the mornings. They ran missions in the Persian Gulf at night and depended on catching up on sleep during the day. We had guys who worked twenty-four-hour shifts as well, but that didn't stop us from the watching the World Series.

In Game Four, Yankees catcher Jorge Posada let a ball slip through his legs in the late innings, allowing the Diamond-backs to score the game-tying run. The Yankee haters in the barracks went nuts.

"You fucking suck, Posada!"

"Go home, Posada, you fucking fuck of a fuck!"

From over the wall, the SEALs woke up cranky.

"Hey, shut up over there!"

Full of confidence, we responded.

"No, it's the fucking World Series!"

"Hey! We work at fucking night! Let us sleep!" they yelled.

Then our supply sergeant, a Yankee fan and quite possibly the least intimidating member of the company, let loose:

"We have guys that work at night, too. *You* shut the fuck up! Why don't you come over here and stop us!"

Later that morning, two SEALs came over and asked to speak to the guy in charge. Bobby Whitesocks was the senior-most man in the barracks at the time, so he got out of his bed and spoke to them. Both of them, he later reported, looked like they couldn't wipe their own asses on account of their arms being so huge.

Bobby defused the situation, managed not to get his ass kicked, and the SEALs left. For good. Two days later, they moved out of our barracks and into new bunks two buildings away.

The fun police eventually defeated us, however, when a bunch of colonels and majors moved in next to us and complained about everything from our television volume to our men speaking in anything more than a whisper when inside. I hated those colonels and majors, a bunch of staff officers who sat in front of computer screens all day. I saw them in the line at the chow hall, most of them overweight and looking like they wouldn't know what to do with a weapon if they were given one. I resisted the urge to yell across the dividing wall that if they worked out in the gym at the end of the day like the rest of us, they would be tired enough to fall asleep at night. Because I was only a lieutenant, I instead waited until night, when all the lights were out, and led the platoon in guerilla warfare—lobbing tennis balls over the partition wall, hoping to hit one of those fat majors as he slept on his bunk. Every time we heard an "ow!" or "shit!" after we threw something across, Ray and I would high-five in the dark.

My men were forced to move the television outside, where they would watch their movies in the cold Kuwaiti night, their poncho liners wrapped around them to stay warm. Once an overweight female sergeant walked over and tried to yell at some of my men about their noise and I just lost it, yelling at her to get the fuck away from my men before I ripped up one of the picnic tables and beat her with it. Stunned, she walked off, and if she ever complained about me, I never heard anything about it.

The officers and sergeants who ran Camp Doha blamed everything on us, from the litter on the streets to the lack of food in the dining hall. They were all support soldiers who worked indoors, and they looked down on my men, whom they dismissed as "grunts," as if my men should be kept in a cage until it was time for them to fight. The only real release we got was when we trained far away from the camp in the desert.

One day at an abandoned satellite compound, three of us climbed to the top of a 120-foot satellite dish and dropped our pants to moon the cameras below as we stood on the thin I-beam. On a dare from one of the guys up there with me, I performed ten picture-perfect pull-ups while hanging from the top lip of the dish. It was just one of the many stupid things I did while in Kuwait, but I was rewarded with the ultimate compliment later when I overheard one of my soldiers tell another soldier in the company, "Lieutenant Exum is fucking nuts. I would follow that crazy fuck anywhere."

Later that night, after we had completed the exercise at the satellite dish, the guys jumped me again, tying me up in the sand with parachute cord and duct tape. They won easily this time, having ambushed me after I completed my day's end speech to them before we left to return to Camp Doha. Afterward, Flash found a knife and climbed on me, sheepishly grinning as he cut me loose from my binds before helping me into the General Lee, where he had already gathered my rucksack, helmet, and equipment.

The way you beat dissention and create motivation in regular army units like my platoon in the Tenth Mountain is by establishing trust first. Motivating troops can be the toughest task a leader faces, especially when those troops are away from home, or in bad weather, or tired and hungry. I have learned, though, that you can build up favors with the men you lead. If you go out of your way to help them when you can, they are more likely to suck things up and follow your lead when things get ugly. With my platoon, for example, I got personally involved in seemingly mundane matters like making sure my soldiers got their proper pay. They returned my efforts by following me when I led.

I found that taking the time to get to know your men well goes a long way. In Kuwait, I would often just sit around and bullshit with the guys—about their hometowns, about their girlfriends, about how much Kuwait sucked, about anything. Every soldier has a story to tell, and if you let him tell it and take interest in what he has to say, he's more likely to listen to you when you brief him on something important later.

This is the human element of leadership. It would be easy to demand soldiers follow your lead solely because of the rank on your collar, but such a style tests a soldier's discipline at the highest level, and eventually he gets sick of it. American soldiers are too independent for the "follow me because I'm in charge" style of leadership.

On the other hand, you don't have the time as a leader to explain everything to everyone every time you make a decision. So you must work to build up trust beforehand. You build trust by massing a track record of past good decision-making and by connecting on a human level with every man you lead. Being physical and fighting the men in the sand was all part of this. It meant a lot to them that I would take off my officer's rank and wrestle with them, one-on-one or all together. There's a physical connection, like when an older brother not only tells his little brother that he's proud of him but also puts his arm around him when he says it. I never hesitated to join my men in their chicken fights with each other, hoisting McCauley's tiny assistant gunner Tayo onto my shoulders as we fought with another pair until one pair fell to the ground, defeated. My men understood me as an officer, as the one in charge, but also as one of their peers, someone who was a soldier just like them, and a human just like them.

This was my style of leadership, and thankfully, I shared it with my platoon sergeant, Sergeant Montoya. But some sergeants and officers questioned my style and told me so. They said I openly cared too much about my men. They said I shouldn't ever explain my decisions—that my soldiers should just execute my orders on the spot because that's what good soldiers should do. But I believe that philosophy is hopelessly outdated, and we have the draft-dodging generation before us to partially thank for it. (After all, if you don't have to fight for your country when she calls you, why should you have to obey every order you're given when you *have* answered the call?)

The most striking thing to me about Pickett's disastrous Confederate charge at Gettysburg isn't that it happened in the first place but rather than no one on record refused to do it. But that was a different time. Only later when I led an elite Ranger platoon would I never have to explain my actions and orders to my men. The Rangers were disciplined enough to just accept orders and execute them. But even there, my subordinate leaders were so damn good at their jobs that I always took the time out to explain my decisions in case they had a better idea, which they often did.

My leadership style has been validated time and time again, both in training and in combat. When I said "jump," my men jumped. And it wasn't because of the rank on my collar. It was because my men trusted me to make the right decisions and respected my authority. Ultimately, the decision they arrived at themselves was that the odds of our success and their survival were greater when they followed my lead and Sergeant Montoya's than when they did their own individual thing.

At home, I have a collection of plaques on my wall from all the men I've ever led into combat. They are inscribed to me, thanking me for my service. The service they thank me for is not my service to the country, but rather to them. I will never forget the greatest lesson I learned in the army, which is that if you want to lead, you must learn to serve first.

BEFORE LONG, IT was the Christmas season, and I began to receive a lot of packages from folks back home. It was my first Christmas away, and I complained to my friends over e-mail that I would miss being with my family in Tennessee. I didn't dare say anything to my mother or any of the other women in the family, as I knew they were more heartsick than I was and would be having a tough enough time as it was. Indeed, once I returned, I heard all about how my mother and aunts and grandmother and sister and cousin had broken down in tears *in unison* during the Christmas Eve service back at Brainerd United Methodist in Chattanooga. I jokingly chided my mother when I returned that they had hardly lived up to the stoic ideal of the Spartan women. But I was lonely during the holidays myself, and wrote to my buddy Mark in Chicago how I would miss the Christmas Eve toasts of single malt scotch at home most of all.

In response, Mark sent me a package just before Christmas with two novels he thought I might enjoy and a flashlight to read them by. I fiddled with the flashlight for a minute before I realized the batteries were dead and needed replacing. But as I took the flashlight apart, out dropped not two D-Cell batteries but a small bottle of scotch. On Christmas Eve, my surrogate family—Ray, Sergeant Rod, and me—gathered for a midnight nip of scotch. I'm sure it pleased Mark to no end that, from thousands of miles away in Illinois, a Jew from Chicago had saved my Christmas in Kuwait.

WE WOULD STAY close to five and a half months at Camp Doha. By the time we left, I knew the roads and deserts of that country like the back of my hand. My favorite times were when we dressed in civilian clothes and went downtown, and I was temporarily able to fool myself into thinking that I was a tourist on vacation rather than a soldier on a wartime mission. Although we all spoke disdainfully of Kuwait and our existence while we were there, as I look back on it I find myself with as many good memories as bad. I went out of my way to experience as much of the country I was living in as I could. I delighted in dragging Flash, Ray, and Sergeant Lane, one of

Ray's team leaders, through the fish market, where all the fish heads and stench and slime hit you full on. To me, that was a real experience, and you couldn't get that at McDonald's or Applebee's or any of the other American restaurants in Kuwait, where Filipino waitresses took orders from Western-dressed and Western-aspiring Kuwaitis sitting with their families among military personnel and expatriates desperate for something familiar in the midst of a foreign land.

We wandered into the bazaars and shops and markets, talking to shopkeepers in pidgin English, taking pictures of the "Gorge Bush Barbershop" (sic) across from—of all things—a Dairy Queen, and sampling the knockoff Rolexes and Tag Hauer watches. We stepped into a shop smelling strongly of spices and fried meats, trying to order whatever it was the guy in front of us just had. I pointed to different things and held up my fingers to communicate how many I wanted to buy as the guy across the counter smiled wide along with me and laughed at our common inability to speak each other's language. From the looks of the rest of the people in the shop, I think we were the first pale-skinned foreigners to step foot in there in a long time, but they were happy to serve us, giving us Pepsis to wash our food down with.

We would sometimes run into British soldiers in Kuwait City who looked as conspicuous as we did. We tried not to stand out, though, so when we ran into other servicemen, we always greeted them with a silent nod like we were spies and didn't want to blow our cover. We blended in as easily as we could for guys pushing or exceeding six feet, mostly white, and dressed in blue jeans, among the shorter Arabs in their traditional dress. We would eventually make our way back to the mall, where I would buy a copy of that week's *Economist*, the only magazine we could reliably get each week, and meet Ray and Sergeant Lane in the espresso shop on the first level, where we drank strong Arabic coffee and stared at all the beautiful Western-dressed Arab women shopping in Benetton or Victoria's Secret before putting their veils back on to head home. Those were good times, and we always bought a few Cuban cigars to enjoy on the way back to base.

In February, our battalion commander came to see us. He had just been to Afghanistan, where he had visited another company in the battalion that had deployed to Uzbekistan and Afghanistan just before Christmas. The BC reported that everyone in Afghanistan was well and doing pretty much the same missions we were, guarding a base and escorting convoys. The real fighting, he guessed, was over, but they were planning one last operation before returning home in April or May.

That operation kicked off at the beginning March. The generals named it "Operation Anaconda" after the Union strategy of strangling Confederate strongpoints like a snake during the Civil War. The target was one last bastion of al-Qaeda fighters who had holed up in the Paktia province to the southeast of Gardez, which in turn was just south of the Afghan capital, Kabul. It was the densest concentration of al-Qaeda fighters in Afghanistan—believed to number several hundred. A few months earlier, al-Qaeda had similarly gathered at Tora Bora to the southeast, but when the allied generals tried using Afghani fighters against them, the Afghanis broke and ran from the more battle-hardened and dedicated al-Qaeda forces. The rumors speculated that Osama bin Laden himself had escaped in the failed operation. This time would be different. American troops—including regular army units—would fight alongside the Afghanis.

The operation began on the second of March. Rifle companies from the Tenth Mountain Division helicoptered into the Shah-e-Kot Valley alongside two battalions from the 101st Airborne Division, allied Afghan fighters, and a host of special operations soldiers that included U.S. Rangers, SEALs, Green Berets, and a small contingent of tough Australian Special Air Service (SAS) operators.

The first twenty-four hours did not go well. The assault by Afghan soldiers broke down immediately under a hail of al-Qaeda mortar and machine gun fire just as it had in Tora Bora. Without the Afghanis to worry about, the al-Qaeda forces, mostly hardened ideologues and experienced fighters, turned to the Americans landing to the south. Two companies from the Tenth Mountain Division were torn up in the opening hours of the battle, hacked apart by accurate and plentiful al-Qaeda mortars. The Americans were forced into a tactical retreat of sorts, bringing the two companies that had come under fire back to Bagram momentarily, evacuating the wounded, and sending the two companies back to another piece of terrain in the valley, out of al-Qaeda mortar range. Meanwhile, the al-Qaeda fighters, rather than running away, streamed into the valley, leading allied intelligence experts to conclude that there must be some "Tier One personalities" in the valley leading them, maybe even including bin Laden himself.

After hearing this news in Kuwait, Captain Rogers fired off a secure e-mail message to the high brass in Afghanistan, telling them we weren't needed in Kuwait and were ready to fight if and when called for. Over the past month, we had been the bastard children of Camp Doha. A military police company had arrived to replace us, but the brass at Doha liked having us around and wouldn't release us. The Tenth Mountain Division couldn't do anything about it because, technically, we no longer belonged to the division and instead belonged to the army's Central Command. In the first few hours of the battle, we got all our information by watching Fox News on the satellite television and hitting the fat staff officers up for information in the dining hall. We groaned every time the television reported another casualty or downed helicopter, sure that we could make a difference if we were there, and heartbroken that we were not.

The low point during Operation Anaconda took place on the fourth day of the month. We watched on the news as the first reports of helicopters being downed flashed across the screen. A Navy SEAL, Chief Petty Officer Neil Roberts, had fallen out of his Chinook helicopter as it came under fire over the Shah-e-Kot Valley onto a mountain called Takur Ghar. In response, a platoon of U.S. Rangers crash-landed onto the mountain to rescue Roberts, unaware that Takur Ghar was an al-Qaeda stronghold. In the ensuing fight, three U.S. Rangers and three other special operations soldiers gave their lives trying to save Roberts. At the time, we were told Roberts himself died in an attempt to fend off the al-Qaeda who quickly surrounded him on the mountain.

The battle wasn't going as well as the generals had hoped, and allied planners began to get the sinking feeling that they didn't have enough forces on the ground to pull off a victory.

Our battalion's company in Uzbekistan was called into service, thrown into the battle as soon as they arrived in Afghanistan. And against all expectations, headquarters called and instructed us to have our company in Afghanistan within twenty-four hours.

Chaos ensued. The barracks erupted in cheers when the news went out that we would be deploying to get in the fight. I sent off five hasty postcards, to my mom, dad, and friends in the States. Guys threw out everything they couldn't fit into bags. I sent three boxes of crap home and packed only what I would need for combat, along with two or three books and my Walkman. We hastily rearranged the barracks, which had taken on the look of a Gypsy camp since we arrived. Guys had strung shower curtains and ponchos between beds to give themselves the illusion of solitude and privacy. Now we pushed all the bunk beds and wall lockers back to their original places along the concrete floors. It caused a fearsome racket, all done in the middle of the night, but when people shouted above the din from across the walled partitions, our men just shouted back spirited "fuck you"s and threw things over the wall at the complainers.

Once everything was packed, we made one last trip to the airport, this time escorted by others, finally the ones with smiles on our faces. But we weren't going west toward home. We were going east, flying over Pakistan into the abyss of Afghanistan. It was dusk as we loaded the plane, putting in earplugs to drown out the whine of the engines of the C-17 and propping our feet up on our rucksacks for the long flight into Central Asia.

I sat next to Bobby and have a picture of the two of us on the plane, smiling for the camera. I noted that it looked like our soccer team was going to miss our end-of-season tournament, which was a pity since we were the number-one seed. Bobby just laughed. We were giddy with enthusiasm, finally released from the tedium of Kuwait and the desert.

IX

WHEN WE GOT off the plane a few hours later, it was dark. The C-17 crew instructed us to disembark quickly so that they could take off again soon. These were the days when snipers with high-powered rifles and rocket launchers were firing at every plane flying into Bagram Airbase—a former Soviet base left over from the wars of the 1980s—as they took off and landed. To counter this, the air force kept their flights confined to nighttime and performed what they called "tactical" landings and takeoffs, in which the plane corkscrews both on the way down and on the way up to avoid incoming fire.

My first memory of Afghanistan was the thick, cold darkness. We couldn't see a thing once we left the plane, and we blindly followed a guide to a tent where we were told to sign in with our names and units. Flashlights were kept to a minimum, and everywhere we walked, we were loudly warned not to step over the white engineer tape where the ground had not yet been cleared of land mines. Our arrival reminded me of the scene in the movie *Apocalypse Now* where Martin Sheen's boat crew first arrives at Colonel Kurtz's lair and is greeted by a manic Dennis Hopper shouting, "There's mines over there! Mines over there too! And watch those goddamn monkeys, they'll bite ya!"

I took my night vision monocle out of my pocket and began to scan the landscape around me. I could make out the faint lights of the control tower as well as a few buildings, and I described what surrounded us to the men around me.

Tired from a long day and night of travel, we marched to a long, bombed-out building with a sign that read MOTEL 6 painted by the entrance. This was the headquarters of the battalion from the Tenth Mountain Division already in Afghanistan, along with one of the companies from my battalion, the Polar Bears.

The folks from our sister battalion were more than accommodating, happy to see friendly faces sporting the same unit patch on their sleeves, giving us coffee and filling us in on how the fighting to the south was going. They had suffered heavy casualties in the opening hours of the fight a few days earlier, and many were back at Motel 6 resting and recovering before they went out again. Others wore bandages from shrapnel wounds suffered during the mortar attacks.

They let us put down our sleeping pads in the darkened hallways, and I fell asleep next to a satellite television they had set up. In one of the many surreal moments I experienced in that country, I struggled to fall asleep my first night with Katie Couric blathering on in New York on the *Today* show.

The next day we woke up and made our way to the mess tent, where we ate orange eggs and drank thick grape juice. Surprisingly, it tasted great, and we hungrily consumed our rations while standing at long high tables they had erected for us in the tent. As we left, we threw our trays in the trash and each grabbed an MRE out of the box by the door for our lunch.

Having only seen the landscape of Bagram and northeast Afghanistan at night, it was a shock to see it during the day. The sun rose from the east over the Hindu Kush and spread light onto another giant mountain range to our west. It was breathtaking. My soldiers who skied gazed in awe at the snowcapped mountains and pointed at the bowl formations where they thought they might find prime skiing. But it was also easy to see why the old Soviet military had met disaster after planting their largest airbase here.

Bagram sat squarely in the middle of the Panjir Valley. It was here in this valley that the legendary mujahideen leader Ahmed Shah Masoud had ambushed the Soviets time and time again, using the tight mountain passes as natural escape routes. In the tribal wars that followed, Masoud had made some of his toughest stands against the Taliban in the valley, which remained sympathetic to the Northern Alliance even after Taliban assassins killed Masoud the day before 9/11.

The rest of my platoon was due to arrive in twenty-four hours on a later flight, so Captain Rogers sent me out to scrounge up any supplies we might need. We especially needed lamination paper to put on all the new maps we were getting, as well as plywood and planks to make a floor for our new tent. Captain Rogers had already spoken to some of the officers at the brigade tactical operations center, and it looked like we were going to be thrown into the mix as soon as we were ready.

This didn't spare Captain Rogers the wrath of the brigade commander. To move our company from Kuwait, Captain Rogers had appealed directly to the division headquarters under the assumption that because he was technically no longer in his regular chain of command, his normal chain of command did not apply. Our battalion commander, a reasonable guy, had made the same assumption and understood Captain Rogers jumping the chain. The brigade commander, however, did not. For a while, I was fearful that he would fire Captain Rogers and put the rest of us to work guarding the base until a new commanding officer could be found. Thankfully, he didn't, choosing only to give him a first-class ass-chewing instead. I think it irked the brigade commander, a man of no small ego, that one of his company commanders had embarrassed him by sneaking our company into combat without his approval.

I spent my time that day wandering our new home, making friends and gathering supplies. I was largely unsuccessful finding the equipment we would need, but I did succeed in getting one roll of lamination paper and enough plywood for Greg and me to start making a floor for our tent. I had bought three logs of Copenhagen snuff in Kuwait to trade in Afghanistan, and I used it to barter for the supplies. I'm a horrible carpenter, but Greg was competent, and between the two of us we assembled a rather tidy plywood floor, raised just enough to let the water flow beneath. In between hammering planks down to cover over the sand, I anxiously waited for my platoon to arrive.

By the time they got there, we had already erected their tents. Captain Rogers made all the platoon leaders stay with him in the planning tent, which meant I was separated from my men. This angered me, because in Kuwait, I had grown used to staying with the platoon and sleeping in a cot near Sergeant Montoya and the squad leaders. But the new arrangement made it easier to plan with the other officers for our upcoming missions. Greg and I seemed to spend most of our time holding the tent together. We were right next to the flight line, so every time a helicopter took off, our tiny tent would threaten to blow away. Even when the tent pegs all held, the tent filled with a thick dust blown in by all the rotor wash. I was assigned to assemble the stove—our only source of heat—and keep it running, while Greg set about building a pull-up bar outside the back door of the tent. Between the amount of weight I would lose in Afghanistan and the frequent pull-ups I did outside the tent on a daily basis, I was able to do almost thirty perfect pull-ups by the time we left. On a bet with one of my soldiers, I once did ten pull-ups with one of the platoon's machine guns strapped on my back.

Before my platoon's first mission, a foray into the south to secure a small helicopter landing zone, I had to pay a visit to the division headquarters, a giant converted airplane hangar with a series of armed guards and checkpoints protecting the innards from attack by lone gunmen or suicide bombers. After waiting for a few minutes, the guards finally let me into the Operations Control Center, where I sought out someone who could help me get some satellite imagery of our objective.

The control center was busy, and no one there was ranked anything less than a captain, so my officer status didn't matter much. I was just an anonymous platoon leader, a peon in the big game unfolding on the series of screens and computer monitors in front of me. I grabbed a captain with military intelligence insignia, however, and explained to him my situation. He seemed busy and annoyed by my intrusion. But before he could go, I noticed the ring on his right hand, the one with my old college dormitory on the side.

"When did you graduate from Penn?" I asked.

"1995" was his startled response.

I put my hand out. "Andrew Exum, class of 2000."

The intelligence captain displayed a wide grin on his face and shouted out for someone to help me with the imagery I had asked for.

"Get this lieutenant whatever he needs," he instructed.

I walked out of the operations center with several spools of satellite photos and a better set of maps than we had been given so far. Captain Rogers was amazed as I dropped the maps onto his bunk, and asked where I had gotten all of it. I just smiled and told him not to worry about it.

I had a lump in my throat as our helicopter took off from the airbase for the first time. If Afghanistan was the Wild West, Bagram Airbase was the equivalent of an old cavalry post, and a safe one at that. Everything outside of Bagram, and the similar bases near Kandahar, Kabul, and Mazar-e-Sharif, was Indian Country.

It was nearing dusk when we left in a Marine Corps CH-53 Sea Stallion that was crammed with the majority of my platoon. On this mission, we would land a few miles to the west of the Shah-e-Kot Valley in order to secure the FARP (Forward Arming and Refueling Point). Before and after helicopters entered the valley, they would stop at the FARP to pick up extra ammunition or fuel. Our mission was to secure the FARP while a demolitions team recovered some Hellfire missiles that had been left there a few days earlier.

I did not expect too much enemy contact, if any. But we were flying into a FARP that had been abandoned just twenty-four hours earlier after intelligence discovered it had become a target for al-Qaeda. Before I left, I ran into a buddy of mine in the 101st Airborne, a tough, smart lieutenant I had attended the Infantry Officer Basic Course and Ranger School with. In a former life, he had fought in the Battle of Mogadishu with the 3rd Ranger Battalion of *Black Hawk Down* fame and was now an officer. He had similarly heard that the FARP had become a target and warned me to be careful. The only thing left there were the missiles, though, so I figured we wouldn't be on the ground for long.

A few hours earlier, I had walked up to the tent housing all the marine aviators who would be ferrying us to the FARP and then bringing the missiles back. As I walked in, I introduced myself to the marine major lounging on the lawn chair by the door bare-chested and wearing sunglasses. I briefed him on our mission, and he shrugged as if he could care less. His job, he explained, was just to fly the chopper. He was a brand of antiquated cool right out of 1968. The only thing missing was some Jimi Hendrix on the stereo.

Aviators responsible for carrying troops into combat are an odd breed, one that always has one foot in combat and one foot keeping a distance from the fray, flying from safety to war and back again. In training, we foot soldiers were often frustrated by aviators who refused to risk their expensive helicopters in inclement weather. With sarcasm, we reasoned that it must be nice to wake up and decide not to fly or fight because of some rain in the forecast. Foot soldiers have no such option. No matter the weather, we have to go. While we sit in a downpour, our boots buried in soft mud, the pilots wait in their hangars for the skies to clear.

This dynamic seems to change in combat. The number of stories chronicling the bravery of pilots swooping in to rescue wounded soldiers in the heat of battle is astronomical. When the game is on the line, pilots can always be counted on. And with respect to the fragility of helicopters, it is telling that more of my friends who have died in the army were killed in peacetime training accidents aboard helicopters than in actual combat. The first soldiers who died in the Afghan conflict perished when a helicopter crashed in Pakistan, not at the hands of an al-Qaeda sniper. One of the men who died was a kid who had been through Ranger School with me. So perhaps the caution of aviators is warranted.

The CH-53 helicopter would not hold the whole of my platoon, so I left one squad behind at Bagram. The explosives experts who would load up the Hellfire missiles—or destroy them if necessary—rode on the second helicopter, which also carried extra fuel. Taking off from Bagram that evening in the early March of 2002, we got our first look at the Afghan landscape from above. The sun was beginning to set in the west, and thus illuminated the crags of the Hindu Kush to the northeast. The helicopter began to rise almost immediately after we left the base, and crested over a large hill to the south.

We then headed due south, passing just to the east of the capital city of Kabul.

After an hour-long ride, we landed and set to work. The FARP site was on a wide-open bowl surrounded by hills anywhere from a mile to five miles in the distance. I began by directing where I wanted the two machine guns placed. The M-240B machine guns held the majority of my platoon's firepower. They had a maximum effective range of around twelve hundred meters and could spit out 7.62mm bullets at a frightening pace. Just one of those bullets would stop a man dead in his tracks. An eight-round burst would saw him in half. I put the guns at the six and twelve o'clock of the helicopter, about three hundred meters from the bird itself.

When setting a perimeter, one of the tricks we used was the clock face. Everyone knows what a clock face looks like, so if you tell a soldier to go to his three o'clock, he instinctively knows to face to the right and walk however far you tell him to march. My first squad occupied the left side of the clock face while my second squad took the other side. My squad leaders placed themselves at the nine o'clock and three o'clock positions respectively. Sergeant Montoya stayed with Gun 2—McCauley and Tayo—at the six o'clock.

I identified a few potential threats to the FARP, one coming from a town about three kilometers from Gun 1 at the twelve o'clock, the others being two small groups of houses about a kilometer from both the seven o'clock and three o'clock. All three of the potential threats looked benign—we could see fires starting in the town as night fell, a sign that the residents were settling down for a quiet evening—but an old Toyota pickup truck with a machine gunner in the back could conceivably close upon our position very quickly from any direction and cause a lot of damage before we could do anything about it.

I walked the perimeter, dragging Flash and his radio along with me and looking at the positions, feeling sorry for the guys on the left side of the clock face who were in the middle of the flat ground with nothing for hundreds of meters to seek cover behind. At least the guys on the right side of the perimeter had a berm to position themselves behind.

Sergeant Montoya, McCauley, and Tayo were keeping busy at their position watching an Afghani man standing on a hill a few hundred meters away from us. They viewed him with suspicion, but to all appearances he was just a curious man observing the spectacle below. I can only imagine what a sight we were for him.

Before I knew it, the helicopter was loaded and ready to go. I called all the men in and boarded the bird myself after the last man stepped in. On the return, I rode in the back and—with my night vision monocular down on my eye—watched the country unfold beneath me. I watched the static electricity swirl around the rotors of the helicopter behind us, loaded with fuel and the rockets, and made out the shapes of roofless farmhouses and huts as they swiftly passed beneath us. To the west, I could once again make out the outskirts of Kabul by the light it gave off in the night, magnified by my night vision. Finally we landed at Bagram, where I led the platoon off the helicopter and we were met by Captain Rogers.

It had been an easy mission. Nothing had gone wrong—no shots were even fired. I walked into our tent, took my boots off, and sat down on my cot. Flash came by to pick up my hand grenades, which we kept in a separate tent for fear one would accidentally have the pin pulled and go off. Our tents were cluttered enough as it was without hand grenades for people to trip over.

I had hoped this mission would be a good dry run for the platoon. I thought that the younger guys would take from the mission the experience of going out into the wilderness and coming back unscathed, which might build their confidence.

I knew we would need all the confidence we could muster in the mission to come.

X

As we returned, I found Captain Rogers was busy planning the first company mission. We were to be attached to a Canadian infantry battalion, the 3rd Princess Patricia's Canadian Light Infantry. ("What the fuck kind of name for an infantry battalion is that?" McCauley demanded.) The plan was for the PPCLI along with our company to lead an assault by helicopter on the Whale, a ridge running north to south on the western edge of the Shah-e-Kot Valley. The al-Qaeda fighters still on the Whale were estimated up to a hundred and were among the most hardened of the fighters remaining in the country.

By this stage of the war in Afghanistan, almost all the Taliban forces had either been killed or had defected to the allied forces. The fighters who'd stayed behind were believed to be either hardcore ideologues or volunteer soldiers from countries they could no longer return to. This included soldiers from the Uzbek Liberation Front in Uzbekistan, Chechen rebels come down from the north, and Arabs from across the Middle East who journeyed to Afghanistan to fight alongside the Saudi, Osama bin Laden, and his Egyptian deputy, Alman al-Zawahiri.

The thought of ideologues with nothing left to lose made me queasy, but not as much as the intelligence revelation that our operatives were beginning to find textbooks in the valley where some al-Qaeda fighters, living with their families, had begun to teach their children from a curriculum we Americans were unfamiliar with. The textbook went something like this:

CHAPTER 1: *Basic Arithmetic*
CHAPTER 2: *Arab Grammar*
CHAPTER 3: *How to build a pipe bomb*
CHAPTER 4: *How to ambush an infantry column*

This new revelation changed our perception of the battlefield because it forced us to consider for the first time that eleven-year-olds we came across might be combatants just as dedicated to killing us as their fathers were. This made young teenagers and even children a potential threat. Privately, we were told that everything on the Whale could be considered a target. "Kill everyone you see" was the rule of the day.

My thoughts on the upcoming fight were that this was going to be an ugly affair. I fully expected to suffer casualties within our platoon and steeled myself for that reality. Before we got onto the helicopters, we had a prayer led by a chaplain and asked God for protection. I wasn't comfortable with the mass prayers and decided I would say my own when I got on the bird. I looked across the company at Ray. While everyone else was bowing down before God, Ray sat on his rucksack, staring across the airstrip, waiting for the show to start.

There were media on the flight line, newspaper and television journalists interviewing soldiers both Canadian and American as they prepared to ride into battle. A pretty French reporter walked up to me and started quizzing me on our upcoming operation in heavily accented but fluent English, and I started in, doing my best to explain what we were about to do without giving away any of the specifics of the company's mission while sounding as much like John Wayne as possible—tough, confident, brave. Inside I was a wreck, though, filled with uncertainty and anxious to start our mission.

When the helicopters were ready, I called my "chalk" to attention. (A chalk is one helicopter load of soldiers, and I was the senior man on my chalk.) After I yelled for Chalk Three to get on their feet, a cameraman from CBS ran over and kindly asked me to say again what I had just yelled. Apparently, the microphone hadn't picked it up the first time and what I had shouted sounded sufficiently sexy to record for the viewing audience back home. One of my sergeants yelled that we were going to be in the air for an hour, so if any of the men needed to piss, they should do so now. About ten guys turned around, whipped out their cocks, and began to piss, right there, on the side of the flight line.

The pretty French reporter looked aghast and turned to me with horror in her eyes. I could only stutter, "Ah, *c'est la guerre, mademoiselle.*" And with an *"au revoir"* I walked the guys to our waiting helicopter.

The first problem we had faced in preparing for the mission was the loads we were asked to carry on our backs across rocky terrain at almost ten thousand feet of altitude. Ninety-pound rucksacks are painful enough in most conditions, but at that altitude, they were insufferable. One of the ways we invented to deal with the weight problem was to load all of our heavy 60mm mortar rounds onto our M-Gator, a John Deere ATV with a cart on the back. The only problem that remained was how to drive the M-Gator on and off a helicopter. Getting on turned out not to be so much of a problem, but the helicopter crew chief made us load the M-Gator at the back of the helicopter. Once we landed, Sergeant Montoya would have to drive it off.

After a nerve-wracking ride south to the valley, during which several of my men puked from the fear of what they were about to face, we had neared our destination. Our helicopter was the third and last in the company to land on the ridiculously small landing zone at the top of the southernmost peak on the Whale. This made me nervous as we hovered in the air waiting for the other birds to land and deposit their loads. We were sitting ducks for anyone who might want to take a shot at us. Out the window I could see Canadian infantrymen lying on their bellies, unsure of whether to scan their sectors for bad guys or shield themselves from the massive amounts of dust and rock being spit up from the helicopter rotor wash.

When it came our turn to touch down, the pilots put us down onto an absurd precipice. Only one out of the helicopter's four wheels actually touched the ground. The crew chief dropped the ramp, and Sergeant Montoya stepped on the ATV's gas, sliding the M-Gator down the ramp and almost rolling it down the mountain before he got it under control. The rest of us poured out the back of the chopper and immediately fell on our asses, skidding down the steep rocky incline. I watched as several of my soldiers fell over and began to tumble head-over-heels down the mountainside. I reached out and grabbed Flash as he began to slide down with our radio.

Once the helicopter took off, I checked my wrist compass and realized that my point man, Corporal Crosby, was walking in the wrong direction. I ran up and grabbed him.

"Hey, Jackass!" I said with a wink, pointing to my compass. "How about the other way?"

Crosby sheepishly grinned and turned the platoon around.

To our pleasant surprise, we encountered no resistance upon landing. In fact, we didn't encounter any resistance at all on that first day. Instead, we moved the company into a defensive blocking position and waited for night to fall. I tied my right flank in with Greg's platoon and my left flank in with the Canadians.

As we were setting up, one of my guys almost shot an Arab-looking guy who walked up to our position and only stopped his advance when my guy popped up with his rifle, backed up by some guys in his team. I came down and interrogated the man, who spoke solid English. He claimed he was an interpreter working with the Special Forces in the region. I asked for his identification as Sergeant Wallace stood to my side, rifle at the ready, waiting to place two bullets in this guy's ear if he tried to do anything sneaky. Lo and behold, the guy pulled out a California driver's license. Apparently, when the call went out for Arabic speakers after 9/11, this dude from Pasadena answered the call and now had almost gotten himself shot in service to his country as a Department of Defense civilian. Because we had explicitly been told that there were no "friendlies" on the Whale, this was quite a wake-up call for my men, who would be more careful with their trigger fingers from now on.

Once I got my platoon settled in, I walked the length of the position with my squad leaders. We placed an LP/OP (Listening Post/Observation Post) up ahead of our position with a radio. The men there would be able to warn us if anyone approached the main position, and could fall back to our position if attacked. All the things we did, we did according to a platoon SOP that Sergeant Montoya and I had written the summer prior. This allowed everyone to know exactly what he was supposed to do in any mission we were given and saved us a lot of time and effort trying to get everyone on the same page. Our guys carried the little book Sergeant Montoya and I had written in their pockets and could flip to the relevant page when given a mission.

Finally, when everything was set and the first guard shift had begun, I sat down where Flash had set up the radio and was now eating his dinner with Uncle Jesse. I took off my body armor and was in the middle of putting on some long underwear when Sergeant Wallace ran up to tell me that the brigade commander was down by his position and wanted to see me. What the brigade commander, nicknamed "CNN 6" by other officers for his remarkable talent for landing himself on the news, was doing on the Whale, I had no idea. But after quickly throwing all my uniform and body armor back on, I walked down to meet him, and there he was, standing there like a fucking cowboy in nothing more than an LBE (Load-Bearing Equipment—really just a belt and suspenders) and armed with only a 9mm pistol, about eighty-five pounds less than what my men had to carry. Christ, he didn't even have any body armor.

It must be nice, the men cynically noted, to walk around without any of the gear *we* had to carry.

He first demanded to know my name and then asked me if I knew what the piece of metal on the ground was.

Sure, I answered. That was a submunition—a bomblet—from one of the giant bombs our planes had dropped.

"That's a goddamn land mine, Lieutenant," he snarled. Using all his human talent for condescension, he then directed the civilian in blue jeans he had brought with him to explain to me what such a "land mine" could do.

"That would damn near blow you apart," he informed me.

"Is it acceptable for you to lose a man in combat, Lieutenant?" the colonel asked as he set in on me again.

"Well," I reasoned, "I guess if the mission demanded it, sir—"

The colonel cut me off and repeated his question, again, slower and louder.

I caught the hint and answered to the negative.

The colonel then placed his hands on his hips and shook his head, doing his best to appear rueful. He explained to me that they had meant to drop a "Daisy Cutter," a massive bomb, onto the Whale before we landed to incinerate all the bomblets that might go off once troops hit the ground and began to shake the earth on which the bomblets lay. Apparently, these bomblets were pretty sensitive. But they had failed to drop the ordinance, so all the little bomblets dropped earlier that had not exploded were still in place.

I thought to myself, *Hey pal, don't blame me for someone else's fuckup. I wasn't the one who decided to drop my men and I on this godforsaken piece of real estate.*

At this point, Captain Rogers walked down, and the brigade commander commenced chewing *his* ass, though of course he had no control where we placed either.

I walked back up to where Flash sat next to the radio and our equipment. Ray was also there, with a wide grin on his face.

"What a jackass," he said.

For the rest of the evening, until the sun had finally set, we sat at our position keeping Flash and Uncle Jesse amused with our impressions of the pompous brigade commander.

"That's a goddamn land mine, Lieutenant!" Ray thundered into the valley below so the Taliban could hear us.

Just as we were bent over with laughter, we saw the explosion. Off to our east, about five kilometers across the valley, rose the mountains that marked the frontier territory on the Pakistani and Afghan border. The majority of the al-Qaeda fighters were holed up in caves and bunkers in those tight mountain passes. Directly to our southeast was the largest mountain on the horizon. It was near the Ginger Pass, which had been the scene of disaster for the Tenth Mountain Division in the opening days of the battle. The mountain was a giant, dwarfing everything else that we could see.

And as the sun set to the west, pouring darkness onto the valley, the outline of the mountain unnaturally disappeared.

A giant fireball rose up into the air for what must have

been a thousand meters, and it was obvious that the air force had just dropped a Daisy Cutter onto the mountains.

I had never seen an entire mountain disappear before, but this one did, under a giant blossom of fire and then a mushroom cloud of smoke.

Ray and I sat facing each other, astonished by what we had just seen. Who had ever heard of such a thing, a mountain disappearing? But as we looked at each other and then back across the valley, we did what seemed to come natural at the moment.

We began to laugh. We laughed because what we had just seen was ridiculous. We laughed because whoever was on the receiving end of that ass-whipping was now in serious pain. And we laughed because whoever he was, he wasn't us.

I am sure that the falling light, and the way the explosion stood out at dusk, had something to do with how awestruck we were. But there was something else. We had just witnessed an expression of power unlike any the world had known since the Hiroshima and Nagasaki bombings. We had seen the U.S. Air Force fight a mountain and win. Feeling confident that the guardian angels above us would keep us safe from harm through the night, we settled down and starting taking turns getting some sleep.

The rest of the night passed without incident. We heard some shooting forward of our position, where some Canadians were, but we didn't make any contact ourselves. On the left flank, Sergeant Montoya and Gun 2 had struck a deal with the Canadians tied into our position. They had stoves, while we had coffee that came in our MREs. So in the morning, as the result of a fair trade, Sergeant Montoya sat on a hill in

Afghanistan brewing coffee with a Canadian squad before we set out for the day's adventures.

That day, the going was very difficult. The first three hundred meters of the day were all straight uphill at an obscene angle. Our platoon had been at sea level for so long that we were unused to operating in the severe altitude with the heavy rucksacks. One of the young privates collapsed on his back when we reached the top of the Whale, and I had to kick him in the rucksack to get him moving again, shouting that if I wasn't hurting, he sure as hell shouldn't be. After all, I was carrying twenty pounds of plastic explosive in addition to my usual load, I reminded him. But the truth was, I was in pain too, despite all the conditioning we had done in Kuwait. I weighed ten pounds more than I usually do due to all the weight lifting I had recently done, and my legs were in great shape. But by the time I left Afghanistan more than a month later, I would have lost almost twenty pounds from the constant exertion and lack of regular food. Nonetheless, I pressed on, pulling Flash and Uncle Jesse along with me. I guess I moved pretty fast—later Flash confessed that he had cursed my name under his breath as I ran ahead on several occasions and expected him to keep up with his radio.

Our company mission was to clear the spine of the Whale, known as the Whaleback. Meanwhile, the Canadian rifle companies would advance on line with us down the eastern and western slopes of the ridge. In effect, we would be pushing the enemy to the south by slowly and deliberately clearing every inch of the Whale as we moved, seeking out caves and fighting positions that he could use.

Our first task as a platoon was to investigate a possible

cave site about five hundred meters ahead. I advanced the platoon to where we thought the cave should be and then put together a small team to conduct a reconnaissance of the area. We couldn't find anything, so I split the area into sectors and had the platoon divide up to search all the sectors. We couldn't find any sign of enemy activity.

I was traveling with the lead team when we spotted our first cave. Crosby looked back at me and asked what I wanted to do. Truth be told, I wasn't too sure at the moment. I had not considered the possibility that we would find a cave so small and benign-looking. It didn't appear to house any fighters. So ignoring the battle drill our company had devised for dealing with caves, I told Crosby to take some cover, pulled out a grenade from my ammo pouch, and tossed it into the mouth of the cave.

The subsequent explosion sent dust and rocks flying out of the cave. But the mouth was so small, anyone who was going to clear the cave was going to have to strip down to his T-shirt and crawl inside with a flashlight and pistol, just like in the old Vietnam movies. I asked for volunteers, and the guy who stepped forward was Wakefield, one of the new privates.

I had nothing but respect for Wakefield even before he volunteered for such a dangerous task. He had severely injured his shoulder earlier in Kuwait playing soccer and had been told by the doctors that his best bet for long-term recovery was to be evacuated home for surgery. But risking long-term problems with his shoulder, he refused to leave, sensing that we would deploy to Afghanistan and not wanting to miss out. He was a little bit older than the other privates, as he had served on nuclear submarines for a few years before he left the

Navy and returned home to upstate New York. He had a young wife and child back home, and after working as a bouncer at a strip club to make money, he decided that his career was going nowhere and that the military would once again offer the best option.

This is how Wakefield came to find himself taking off his body armor and helmet, cocking a pistol, and crawling head-first into a cave that day in eastern Afghanistan. I had no guilt about sending Wakefield in there because I would have done the same thing myself if I were a private. In fact, if it had not been for Corporal Crosby helpfully suggesting that perhaps the platoon leader shouldn't be the one crawling through caves and tossing hand grenades, I might have. But I wondered if I would have been as brave as Wakefield with a family back home. It was easy for guys like me to be brave—we didn't have anxious wives and small kids counting on us to return safely.

Wakefield crawled all the way inside the cave, turned on his night vision goggles, and reported back that the cave was clear. So we pulled him out, and Ray came down to help me prepare the demolitions charges.

It is very difficult to seal the mouth of a cave with plastic explosive. C-4 works well when you're trying to cut through metal, but TNT or dynamite is a better explosive for breaking rock. Nonetheless, Ray and I did our best, first packing the mouth of the cave with rocks and then wedging sticks of C-4 into the spaces left over. Our goal was to create an explosive force that would cause the roof of the cave's mouth to collapse. Ray, a former combat engineer, didn't give our charge much of a chance for success.

Only Flash, Ray, and I remained behind to set the charges. Everyone else had retreated to a safe distance. Together, Ray and I pulled the fuse igniters and then scrambled back to where the rest of the platoon was. At first, we were able to move fast. But after only a hundred meters of scrambling up at a high angle, we were winded in the altitude and had to slow to a fast walk. Nonetheless, we were able to reach the platoon before the charge went off. When it did, we were in defilade, safe from the cave's mouth, and so couldn't see the explosion directly. But we heard the loud roar and then watched dirt and rocks fly into the air and against the rock wall across from the cave.

I sent the rest of the platoon back to our assembly area and stayed behind with one squad to check out the damage after the smoke had cleared. Sure enough, we had only succeeded in making the mouth of the cave larger. In the days that followed, two other units would "discover" the cave, and despite my warnings over the radio that my platoon had already cleared and attempted to destroy the cave, the two Canadian units would try to do the same thing with similar results.

As I was walking back up to our assembly area, however, Flash reported that Second Platoon had made contact. I stuck my ear to my radio receiver and monitored the situation. Second Platoon, Greg's platoon, had discovered an al-Qaeda cave complex and were starting a full assault on the position. Soon, however, it became apparent that the position was larger than anyone had previously thought, and so Captain Rogers called on the radio for me to bring forward whatever I had with me. I responded by taking off at high speed across the spine of the Whaleback with my third squad, Sergeant Wallace's. The eight-hundred-meter trek was exhausting. On a running track, I can cover that distance in about two and a half minutes. With a ninety-pound load and at ten thousand feet, however, it took significantly longer. To my rear, Sergeant Wallace was kicking his guys in the ass, trying to get them to move at a run, but he was just as tired as they were. Up ahead, I could hear explosions and the staccato beat of the M240B machine gun. In the sky, I saw the Cobra attack helicopters circling. Above them, you could make out the contrails of A-10 Warthogs, and above them B-52s, circling in the sky. They must have heard the reports of the fighting and were getting themselves in position to attack.

We finally got there ourselves, though one of Sergeant Wallace's automatic riflemen had collapsed along the way and was being dragged forward by Corporal Banducci. So by the time we reached the objective, I had only five men with me besides Flash and Uncle Jesse. I put the men on a line to cut off any al-Qaeda who might try to escape. Then I went forward with Flash and Uncle Jesse to find Greg.

Ahead, the shooting had died down, though I could still hear individual shots being fired. A Canadian sniper team with Sergeant Wallace fired a shot into the valley. Sergeant Wallace asked them what they were firing at as his squad grew anxious and trigger-happy.

"Nothing, bud," came the reply. "Just squeezing a few rounds off."

Flash and I entered the fighting positions. As we did, I turned the corner and put my foot down on something soft. It gave way beneath me. Catching my balance, I looked down to realize that I had just put my boot into the belly of a freshly killed soldier.

The fighter's clothes were dirty and torn. A few yards away was a rifle. Second Platoon must have taken it out of his hands as they moved forward. Where the dead man's face was supposed to be, only a black hole remained. I couldn't help but pause and look into the man's facial cavity. I could not see anything human there. His face had collapsed into nothingness.

I coolly told Flash, "Mind you don't step on the dead guy," trying to sound as if this were the most natural thing in the world.

I didn't bother to look back to catch his reaction. Instead, I reached my arm back and pulled him along.

"Watch yourself, sir!" came a cry from up ahead.

Before us, a "Misfit" from Second Platoon warned me of an unexploded enemy grenade nearby with the pin already pulled. After treading lightly around the grenade, I quickly found Greg and asked him what he needed.

"Just keep your guys in position," he told me. "And bring forward explosives."

The cave complex Greg's platoon had found was large. Rocks were stacked up all along the sides to provide firing positions. Down a bit, the enemy had stashed a cache of medical supplies. Also, there was plenty of rifle ammunition and rockets. In the middle of the position, the guy Greg's platoon had killed had apparently dug a shallow grave for one of his dead buddies. He had not had the time to cover the man up, so Flash and I could see where the corpse's arms and torso had been stacked under a light cloth. We could not see where his legs were, or if the body even had those anymore.

At this point, the men of Greg's platoon were setting charges on all of the equipment they had found and were attempting to seal the main entrance to the cave complex below. Darkness was falling, so once the charges had been set, Greg's platoon began to retreat off the position while my guys stayed behind to cover their movement. Once everyone was off, I looked around the area, checking for anyone we might have missed, and then ordered Sergeant Wallace to get his guys moving. We fell in behind Greg's platoon as we all marched back single file to the positions we would occupy for the night.

Once we had gotten about four hundred meters away, we heard the charges go off. I looked behind me and saw the plumes of smoke rise up into the evening sky.

When I returned to my platoon, I got everyone situated for the night, organizing a perimeter and checking the guard rosters my squads had drawn up. In the platoon command post in the middle of the patrol base, Flash, Uncle Jesse, and I would all share a radio watch through the night. While two men slept, the other would keep his ear to the radio, listening for any alerts or orders from the company.

Out in the darkness, just before the entirety of the sun fell behind the distant hills to the west, I could see a helmeted figure moving toward our position. The guy wasn't wearing a rucksack and was dressed in civilian clothes, blue jeans, and a T-shirt. My guys had allowed him inside the perimeter after briefly stopping him, and once he made his way to me he introduced himself as a reporter from *Newsweek*. He asked if it was safe to hike back to his rucksack from there. I told him that I wouldn't want to make the nearly two-mile hike myself, but that he was more than welcome to do so. I warned him that the odds were greater of him getting lost, or shot by some of the other friendly perimeters he was likely to stumble into in the dark, than of him being accosted by al-Qaeda.

He decided to stay inside our perimeter for the night. He didn't have any food, so I gave him my last MRE, figuring we would get resupplied in the morning. He also didn't have any warm clothes, so Flash gave him his insulated poncho liner. It turned out that the reporter's father was Iranian, and he wasted no time in telling Flash and me how angry he was at the President's recent "Axis of Evil" speech. He came off as cynical and condescending, with a holier-than-thou tone I found typical among the younger reporters covering the war. I wanted to tell the guy where I had gone to school and that I wasn't as dumb as he obviously thought, but I kept my mouth shut, allowing him to typecast me as the uneducated automaton he thought us all to be.

The older reporters weren't as bad. You got the feeling that they were all pretty liberal, but they never let their personal politics get in the way of their reporting as far as I could see. They refused to be condescending toward the soldiers and treated us all with genuine respect. I think some of them were in awe that so many young men would so willingly risk their lives in combat like this. One older reporter, from the *L.A. Times*, would let me use his satellite phone to call home. Another, a CNN correspondent we recognized from the television, used to come sit by the campfire at Bagram and bullshit with my platoon late into the night, trading cigarettes and stories. We egged on the CNN and Fox News guys, asking each if the other was "the al-Qaeda of cable news." They both answered yes without hesitation. And then the CNN guy would laugh. The Fox News guy never did. But he did do PT with us in the morning, causing the guys to snicker at the warm-up tights he insisted on wearing while joining us.

The rest of the media gravitated toward the intense games of platoon-on-platoon kickball we played during our sparse downtime. Lacking any proper sports equipment, we tightly wound a fleece jacket into a ball and covered it with a plastic garbage bag wrapped in thick strips of duct tape. The games primarily served to showcase our considerable individual talents for shit-talking, and the media sat on the sidelines laughing at us and snapping away with their cameras on the rare occasions that we actually made a play. One cameraman, however, was almost run over when he set up for a shot behind third base, a tent peg, just as the runner from second attempted to steal.

The games would only end when it grew too dark to make out the ball in the Afghan twilight.

THAT NIGHT ON the Whale I was awakened by the sound of gunfire. Looking through my night vision goggles, I could make out a small firefight down the ridge between Canadians and some unseen enemy. I heard the *Newsweek* reporter stir a few feet away. I knew he had to be cold even with Flash's poncho liner. The rest of us had sleeping bags, but there was no way the reporter was going to sleep for more than a few minutes at a time as cold as it was.

The next day, we broke camp and gave the reporter some directions before continuing down the ridge. The day passed without incident. It seemed that any al-Qaeda fighters on the Whaleback had fled after their run-in with Second Platoon the day before. We heard the Canadians had been in a few skirmishes down the ridge, but that it hadn't amounted to anything serious. All together, the fight for the Whale had been a cakewalk, much easier than what we had expected.

We started the morning with a much-needed water resupply. It was very tough to bring supplies in to units at the higher elevations, so the helicopters spent as much time dropping off supplies as they did dropping off soldiers. No truck could make it up those steep cliffs, and hiking down the ridge to get water was out of the question. Such an operation would have taken all day.

Around 0900, a Chinook appeared around the bend with an entire crate of bottled water lashed under its belly. Trying to set the crate of water down, however, was proving difficult. In the end, we tried to put it on one of the ridge's flatter peaks. But the wind conspired against us, and as the helicopter set the crate down, it swayed to the side, clipped a rocky outcropping, and fell over. We—including some of us who had not had a drink of water in twelve hours—watched helplessly as a third of the crate broke apart from the nylon webbing holding it together and tumbled down the hill. Still, we had enough to give each man a little over a liter of water, enough to make it for another day so long as we rationed our drinking.

Food was another matter. I had given my last meal to the reporter, and we would not be resupplied with chow until the next day. Some of the soldiers had not eaten in over a day. They were not used to eating less than two meals a day, and

Sergeant Montoya and I chewed out our team leaders for not watching how much the guys were eating. Now they would be fighting both fatigue and hunger in addition to the enemy, all because they had failed to ration their supplies. I chided myself for giving that meal to the *Newsweek* reporter, but reasoned that I had been through far worse hunger pangs in Ranger School.

By noon, my platoon was the southernmost unit on the Whaleback. We had been delayed because the Canadian battalion had not met up with us yet on the sides of the ridge. Some of my guys laughed that they couldn't keep up with our pace. That wasn't true, though—their job clearing the sides of the ridge was much more difficult than ours had been. We all agreed that the Canadians were a hardy, tough, and dependable crew. Most of them were older than the average U.S. soldier. Many seemed to have either dropped out of high school or to have worked in manual labor jobs for a few years before joining the military. We had a good relationship with them, and Captain Rogers was impressed with how intelligent their operations officer was. Their snipers were universally acknowledged to be world-class, and because we were the forwardmost unit, they hung around my platoon, setting up behind rocks and searching through their scopes for any threats.

As the day wore on, my soldiers and I sat behind some rocks on the spine of the Whaleback, waiting for permission to advance to our next objective, about one hundred meters away. I could see through the binoculars the remains of an enemy position and hoped we might get to do some shooting before the day was done. But one hour spent in that position soon turned to two hours, and as the platoon waited in the sun, they grew bored and started searching the cliffs to the west for anyone creeping around the floor of the western valley.

There, two of my soldiers, looking through binoculars, spotted two Canadian soldiers stopping a car traveling south down the rocky dirt road. The car didn't have the markings identifying it as friendly, but the men inside stepped out and didn't appear to my guys to be carrying any weapons. Then a few more Canadians came out from the side of the road, and before my guys knew it, the Canadians had shot the two guys from the car with several bursts from their M-16s.

"Holy shit!" one of my guys exclaimed.

More of us crept over to where my men were watching through binoculars as the Canadians pushed the car off to the side and cleared the road.

When people ask me what Afghanistan was like, I always answer, "Like the Wild West." It was a place where, as Graham Greene wrote of the colony in *The Heart of the Matter*, "human nature hadn't had time to disguise itself." That scene in the valley that day reminds me of how lawless things were. Had the Canadians felt threatened? Did those Afghanis even have weapons?

Admittedly, we couldn't see for sure from that far away, even with binoculars. I wasn't there on the ground. Maybe I would have made the same decision.

A few weeks before I arrived, a buddy of mine was traveling through Afghanistan with a group of his own soldiers and a contingent of Afghani militiamen. These troops were from what was then still known as the Northern Alliance and had not yet merged with the so-called Eastern Alliance to form the

Afghani Military Forces (AMF). These militiamen had been fighting the Taliban for years but were basically still rebels led by warlords. They had neither the discipline of a formal army nor the leadership provided by a professional officer corps.

My friend was the senior U.S. serviceman on the ground, a lieutenant like me and probably no older than twenty-four. The senior Afghani "officer" was a typical warlord type, older and obviously the veteran of many skirmishes and battles. The men with him, though, were much younger, and it wasn't long before my friend's men had captured an Afghani who had tried to steal one of the scopes from a U.S. soldier's weapon. The Afghani warlord took the man by the neck, considered him a moment, and then took him a few feet away, where he put a bullet from his pistol into the thief's temple.

The U.S. soldiers were shocked. They decided they would think again before turning a thief over to the warlord.

Then again, they didn't have any more cases of theft.

That episode was a reminder to my friend and to all who heard the story what kind of country Afghanistan really was. It *was* the Wild West. In a land where anything goes, everything went.

WE DIDN'T HAVE any luck finding any more al-Qaeda on the Whale. My platoon apparently rankled some of the bigwigs, including the brigade commander, who accused Captain Rogers of jeopardizing foreign relations with Canada by outpacing them so badly on our assault over the Whaleback. At one point, I was almost a kilometer ahead of the Canadians' forward units and was sternly ordered on the radio, over much protest, to halt my movement. It was a political decision. There wasn't any threat or reason for me to be more cautious. It just looked bad for the American company to be so far ahead on what was supposed to be a Canadian operation.

The next day, we left the Whale and hiked down the ridge to a small helicopter landing zone.

"This is a landing zone?" asked Sergeant Montoya. "That ain't no landing zone. That's the size of a '66 Mustang. No way they're going to land a helicopter here."

Sergeant Montoya was right. I had no idea how they were going to set down a Chinook for us to climb aboard. To make matters worse, two of the soldiers from our engineer squad had come down hard with what the medics initially diagnosed as altitude sickness exacerbated by dehydration from the night before. One of them had run through several IV bags of fluid during the night, and the medics stayed up with him in shifts to keep him from going into seizures.

As a result, we had to carry both of them down the ridge on litters, which would have been an impossible task if it weren't for the determination of the company's men. Leading the way was Staff Sergeant Rodriguez, my former squad leader, who was now the platoon sergeant for Greg's platoon and would later win the Bronze Star with valor device for his hero-ism a few days earlier in Second Platoon's assault on the al-Qaeda position we had cleared. When Second Platoon's at-tack had stalled in the rocky terrain, Sergeant Rodriguez had rushed to the front, climbed the enemy position, and killed the first enemy fighter at close range with his carbine. Now Sergeant Rodriguez had stripped off his body armor and his equipment and was dragging one of the soldiers down the mountain on a sledlike stretcher with its tether attached to Sergeant Rod's waist. He was exhausted, and by the time my men and I arrived on the scene to relieve him, he was soaked with sweat despite how cool the air was and despite how little water he had drank over the past few days.

We labored hard to carry those men over that terrain for more than a mile. The real ass-kicker was the two hundred meters we had to carry the men straight up to the LZ at the end of the movement. It was inspiring to watch twenty men working in shifts to carry the two stretchers. Once one man grew too tired to carry the stretcher any longer, another was ready to take his place for a minute or two, or however long his forearms could last.

It's tough to find spontaneous teamwork like this outside the military. No leaders were really necessary. The soldiers knew instinctively what needed to happen to carry the men off the ridge, dividing themselves into teams without being told and sensing when a teammate was too tired to carry on and needed a break. Privates took the place of sergeants carrying the stretcher—"Step aside, Sergeant. It's okay, I've got it."—and others followed behind with weapons providing cover for the stretcher-bearers. By the time we reached the LZ, we were all exhausted and now were being beaten across the face with the rotor wash from the helicopter. One soldier leaned over the stretcher to protect the injured soldier's face from the dust.

The helicopters themselves never actually landed. They just dropped their rear ramps while hovering a foot above the ground. We got the wounded on first, while Captain Rogers and I waited to board the last bird. We ducked every time a helicopter came close, its rotors briefly swinging directly above us before the bird rose and came to a state of suspended animation at the crest of the LZ.

And then we were on the helicopter, with me shouting to make sure Captain Rogers had made it aboard and checking that we had not left anyone. I was one of the last on and sat near the ramp with some of my men, watching the Whale disappear behind us.

XI

WHEN WE GOT back to Bagram, the doctors couldn't find anything seriously wrong with the soldiers who had come down with altitude sickness. To be sure, one of the soldiers was suffering from severe dehydration. I rode with him in the back of a Humvee to the surgeon's station, squeezing his IV bag with my hand and forcing fluid into his bloodstream. The physician's assistant sat across from me in the back of the Humvee, monitoring his vital signs. When we arrived at the surgeon's station, located just below the air traffic control tower, four guys carried him on a stretcher into the operating room while I walked behind, the IV bag held high above my head.

The other soldier who had to be carried off the ridge, Weeks, was more of a mystery. The doctors could not identify a single thing wrong with him.

Both soldiers were engineers and slept next to each other

in their tent. When the first soldier had made it back from the surgeon's station and was resting on his cot, he suddenly went into fits, falling into a seizure right there in the tent during the middle of the afternoon. I held him down with another soldier while the medics went to work. A Canadian medic from a few tents away ran over and held his head while the doctors set to work putting in another IV and preparing to evacuate the soldier.

The funny thing was that, as the first soldier went into fits, so did Weeks in the next bunk over. This exasperated the doctors, who threw up their hands and wondered how many soldiers were going to go into seizure while they were in the tent. After all, there had appeared to be nothing wrong with Weeks when we arrived.

Weeks was one of the more gentle soldiers in the company. He was a quiet kid from Virginia who wore glasses, and I had pulled him aside a couple of times when we were in Kuwait to make small talk about the deployment, the army, and life. His mother was his only family and she had been encouraging him to leave the army and return home. He was an awkward kid who possessed no discernible athletic ability or physical coordination. We all played volleyball one afternoon in Kuwait, and the other soldiers laughed as Weeks tried to hit the ball and only succeeded in knocking it thirty meters to the side of the court. He shyly smiled as the other players laughed every time he sliced or shanked the ball out of bounds. The other soldiers weren't deliberately trying to be mean—the sight of Weeks battling the volleyball to no avail was just too comical to bear.

I would spy Weeks reading his comic books alone on his

bunk in the afternoon, and he reminded me of myself at the age of twelve, small and uncoordinated, unable to join in the games of my larger peers, seeking to lose myself in fantasy. But that was eleven years ago. I had grown up since and wondered what was going through Weeks's head here in combat.

In retrospect, I think something snapped in Weeks in Afghanistan. The battalion's physician's assistant took me aside one afternoon and confessed that they had definitively determined that nothing was wrong with him. After putting him through some tests, it was revealed that he suffered from neither dehydration like the other soldier nor altitude sickness. Our guess was that he had seen his friend go down with dehydration, and not have to fight anymore, and had chosen the same route even though nothing was physically wrong with him. To be fair, the engineers had been through a tough stretch on the Whale. Because of all their explosives, they carried more weight than any of us, and they were always in demand. But poor Weeks just couldn't stand the pressures of combat.

Back at Bagram, I learned that one of my own soldiers, Kidd, had suffered a nervous breakdown on the Whale that Sergeant Montoya had kept quiet from the other troops. Sergeant Montoya knew that I would have no sympathy for such a thing in the midst of a combat operation and probably would have flown off the handle had I heard that one of my soldiers had broken down crying one night out there. I know that sounds callous, but too much is at stake in combat for a soldier to simply decide he doesn't want to play the game anymore. I fully expect my soldiers to be scared at times, just as I am, but when one suffers a breakdown in the middle of the battlefield, crying and refusing to fight anymore, he's not only letting his mates down, he's endangering all their lives. The soldier in question was older than the rest, about thirty-two, and was clearly one of the weaker men in the platoon. I know it must have irked him that a soldier twelve years his junior, Crosby, was his team leader, but age isn't a reason for promotion. The Whale proved that, as nineteen-year-olds proved their mettle while Kidd broke down under pressure.

Now, for the rest of our missions, someone else would have to carry Kidd's gear. And losing another engineer to a purported back strain meant that all of us would have to carry the heavy demolitions equipment ourselves and set up the majority of our own explosives as well. The loss of three of our engineers meant that at the times when Ray and I needed to be leading our troops, we would instead be fiddling with detonation cord and C4 in efforts to blow up al-Qaeda bunkers we came across.

When we returned to Fort Drum, it wasn't long before we saw and heard of more of the effects of combat-related stress. One soldier returned home to East Tennessee, about sixty miles from my own home in Chattanooga, and quite literally went crazy. His friends at home found him in the woods days after he was reported missing, covered in mud and hiding behind rocks. When they tried to give him food, he began throwing Chicken McNuggets as if they were grenades, shouting "Fire in the hole!"

Most of these episodes struck me as absurd. After all, the soldier from Tennessee who went crazy never even saw really intense combat. His platoon was the only one in the company that did not register at least one confirmed kill. He never saw the worst of the war—he never even fired his weapon. And while I understood post-traumatic stress disorder I failed to see any traumatizing events that could have affected him so much. Shortly after that soldier was committed to psychiatric treatment, another soldier from our unit went AWOL and—upon resurfacing—blamed the trauma he had been through for his behavior.

"Fucking pussies," I muttered under my breath as the stress-related incidents piled up.

Captain Rogers, however, heard me and said he wasn't so sure. He thought maybe some of the incidents were genuine. I was surprised to hear that coming from Captain Rogers, who wasn't the most empathetic person under normal circumstances. But he reasoned that unlike some, who seemed to thrive on the pressures and dangers of combat, others retreated into a shell, unable to fit the realities of combat into their previously benign and protected American lives.

I was wrong, and I knew it. I was in no position to judge what effects combat trauma had on someone else. Still, I was frustrated. It seemed that whenever a soldier screwed up in the months after we returned, he blamed his misbehavior—whether it was a DUI or a bar fight—on the lingering effect of combat stress.

THE MEDIA DESCENDED like flies after we landed at Bagram following that first mission. They got quotes from all of us, especially the guys from Greg's platoon who had seized the fighting position on the Whaleback.

We now heard the story of how one of Greg's squad leaders, Sergeant Robinson, had burst into a room made of stones and existing rock walls and blasted what he thought was an enemy fighter six times with his shotgun. It turned out the fighter was only a white T-shirt hanging up in the room, but with all the dust, Sergeant Robinson couldn't tell. He just saw what looked like a torso moving toward him through the dust and smoke. We had a good laugh at his expense.

"Meanest damn T-shirt I ever seen," he sheepishly offered afterward.

Another *L.A. Times* reporter—different from the one I had met before—interviewed me for a story he filed that my mother would read the next day after someone sent it to her. He was a middle-aged man of about forty, and I asked him where he had gone to college. He replied the University of Pennsylvania, and I surprised him by informing him I had written for the same campus newspaper he had. He told me that when he was at Penn, no one who worked for the *Daily Pennsylvanian* would have been likely to have served in the military. I laughed and assured him that I was an anomaly, which set him at ease.

After that, a cameraman spied the name stitched on the back of my hat and asked where I was from. It turned out that we were from the same hometown. Not only had we gone to the same prep school, but incredibly, the school had been named after his great-grandfather. His father had been the headmaster when I went through. Elated at our mutual discovery of a fellow East Tennessean in Afghanistan, he let me use his satellite phone to call home like the other *L.A. Times* reporter had a week earlier. But just as with the call placed from the *Times* reporter's phone, no one was home when I called, so the most I could do was leave a message. Our families back home were somewhat close, so he called his father to let him know that I was safe and to pass word to my parents that I was okay. We sat on his bunk sharing his Snickers bars and talking about Chattanooga and our remarkable high school football team, which had won the state championship a few months earlier. Afghanistan was turning out to be a small, small world. When I stepped back out of the tent, I had to remind myself where I was.

We didn't have much time to think about what we had just been through, though. After just a few hours on the ground back at Bagram, we began planning for the next mission, a descent into the roughest section of the Shah-e-Kot Valley. I scurried around Bagram grabbing supplies where I could and helping to laminate our new maps. My platoon was given the "main effort" for this mission. We were chosen to accomplish the most difficult tasks, clearing and destroying enemy forces surrounding two suspected cave sites.

On the first mission, we had doggedly searched the Whale for days, looking for al-Qaeda soldiers, each one of us a little Ahab dressed in Kevlar, destroying a few caves and killing a few bad guys along the way. We had quickly learned that elevation was a killer. You find yourself straining for breath, your rib cage sore at the end of the day from trying to inhale and exhale so forcefully. Soldiers had told us beforehand that 85 pounds of gear would feel like 120 at ten thousand feet. For once, the reality was just as bad as the hype.

The Whale was also the place where CNN had filmed me crawling out of a cave minutes before the cavern disappeared in smoke and dust from the charge of plastic explosives Ray and I had carefully placed inside. The tape the camera crew made was probably only a few hours old when my mother saw it back in Chattanooga. I can't help but wonder if someday I'll watch my own sons fight their wars in real time.

FOR OUR NEW mission we were deploying farther to the east, deep into what the army called the Upper Shah-e-Kot Valley, where the fiercest fighting thus far between U.S. troops and al-Qaeda had taken place. It was where the Navy SEAL Neil Roberts and the six other special operators had been killed.

The bigwigs back at Bagram Airbase, monitoring the battle from cameras in the sky, had seen him fall from the Chinook, they told us. Then they saw Roberts rise to his feet and attempt to flee from the chasing enemy. A firefight ensued. Roberts fought to the end but was captured.

Al-Qaeda didn't kill him, the men at Bagram told us. Not at first. Instead, they tortured him. Only when a team of special operators landed and joined the fight did the al-Qaeda forces end Roberts's life with a 9mm shot to the head.

After hearing that, it's a wonder we didn't commit any war crimes ourselves. After what happened to Chief Roberts, all of us, myself included, were out for vengeance.

The ride into the next mission wasn't nearly as bad as the previous one had been. This time, no one puked from anxiety or airsickness, though the CH-47 Chinooks took the same high-speed, "map-of-the-earth" routes over the mountains south of Kabul into the Paktia province. Each time we crested a ridge, the pilots would let the birds quickly drop down the other side, sending our stomachs up into our necks.

In contrast to the bleak landscapes we had seen so far in Afghanistan, the Upper Shah-e-Kot was beautiful. The mountains towered over us, and the valley itself was greener than the desolation of the Whale. My platoon, as the main effort, was the last to land. The other platoons had been given the mission of clearing our route to suspected cave sites south of the landing zone. As we landed, we heard explosions in the distance. Cobra helicopters buzzed above us scanning for enemy fighters and destroying two bunkers they had spotted to our north with Hellfire missiles. The helicopters gave us red-blooded American confidence that we once again had our guardian angels above us.

We soon began to head south into a streambed, the ridges to our right and left rising sharply. Up ahead the explosions continued. First Platoon had found a cache of rocket-propelled grenades but had thrown a grenade into the cave instead of clearing it properly with plastic explosives, which would have destroyed the missiles completely and safely. Instead the missiles were just on fire, and every so often an RPG would cook off and come screaming over our heads.

Bullets shooting over your head are bad enough. Rockets are worse, and my men were understandably nervous every time one whizzed by. I'm sure every soldier had the same image I had in my mind, of taking one of those rockets to the head and being decapitated.

The danger from the flying rockets became so immediate that I was forced to alter our route westward, out of the streambed. We began to climb the steep ridge. Our platoon advanced single file, not the most secure way to move but the quietest, and the only way the rocky, mountainous terrain was passable.

Eventually we crested the ridge and advanced down the slope toward our objective, the suspected cave, now about eight hundred meters away. We were about three hundred meters from our objective when we spotted the first of many enemy bunkers, in a gulley to our west. I radioed Captain Rogers for permission to halt my column in order to destroy the bunker. He agreed, and I set my men into place.

I felt like the conductor of the world's most violent symphony orchestra. With a wave of my left hand, my men launched an antitank rocket into the bunker. Then with the wave of my right hand, 40mm grenades rained down upon the bunker's roof. The destructive force of these munitions— considered small in comparison to other weapons in the armed forces arsenal—is something so awesome you literally have to see it to believe it. I saw the antitank rocket burst into flames on impact, showering the bunker with its smoke and gases. I watched as the grenades fired from tubes three hundred meters away ripped full-grown trees in half.

Once the dust settled, I quickly scanned the bunker for movement and then tapped the back of my lead machine gunner, Junk. He opened up with his M240B, sending fifty rounds into the front aperture of the bunker. I tapped him again and he stopped.

We waited.

The bunker remained silent. Either the enemy had already gone, they were dead, or they had decided not to answer our call to join the battle.

We continued on down the ridge, spotting another bunker to our west and giving it the same treatment. Finally we arrived within one hundred meters of our suspected objective, and Ray and I moved in for a closer look. We dropped our rucksacks to move more quietly and advanced carefully down the ridge. We didn't say a word, for fear of alerting the enemy—who from the explosions now surely knew we were in the area—to our immediate presence. Instead we sent signals and pointed out to each other with our left hands, never removing our right hands, our firing hands, from the pistol grips of our carbines.

After thirty minutes of searching the area where the cave was supposed to be, we had found nothing. We saw a lot of wreckage where air force bombers had obviously dropped heavy tonnage, as well as some old, uncovered fighting positions with rocks stacked up two feet high for walls. But there was no cave, and no trace of al-Qaeda.

I brought the rest of my platoon forward and organized them into two groups. One group would stay on the ridge and continue looking for the cave. The other group, led by myself and consisting of Ray's squad with an attached machine gun team, would descend into the gulley to the west to search the bunkers we had just cleared and look for others.

Sergeant Montoya stayed on the ridge with Junk and the other machine gun, providing covering fire as we moved through the valley. Junk called this his "Jesus Fire"—that is, fire from above that protects us sinners who march into the valley of death. Junk never ceased to bring a smile to my face, and I trusted him. Probably not enough to loan twenty dollars—but to guard my life, sure.

The first thing we spotted in the floor of the gulley was a mortar cache, which we marked and left for future demolition. As we advanced toward a bunker Sergeant Montoya had spotted through the binoculars, Ray's squad marched up ahead while I moved up the trail with McCauley's gun team, Flash, and Uncle Jesse.

We had worked our way up into some rough, rocky terrain when we spotted the bunker. We weren't sure if it was manned or not. It wasn't one of the positions we had fired an antitank rocket at earlier.

Ray sent a team behind us to guard our rear, and I set to work organizing our assault on the position. After some quick radio coordination between Sergeant Montoya and myself, we attacked. Junk opened up with the gun from high above, peppering the bunker with 7.62mm rounds as Sergeant Lane's team advanced, with Ray eyeing their progress. If there were someone in the bunker, we were counting on Junk to keep their heads down long enough to let Sergeant Lane's team get close enough to toss grenades.

As Sergeant Lane's team got closer, I threw a purple smoke grenade to signal Junk to lift his fire. Junk did so, and the bullets ceased zipping into the bunker. Sergeant Lane then crawled up to it and threw a grenade into the aperture. The bunker shook as smoke bellowed out the entrance. As this was going on, Uncle Jesse shook my shoulder.

In his North Georgia twang he yelled, "Sir, I thank there's a position behind us." I spun around and saw what he was talking about. To our rear and up a steep hill, a poncho hung in the trees above what looked to be a fighting position. If someone was there, Sergeant Lane's team was in the middle of the enemy kill zone with no cover around them.

I yelled to Ray, "I'm going with the gun team to take care of this."

He nodded, and we set off.

I first instructed McCauley to set his gun aside and pull out his sidearm, a Beretta 9mm pistol. McCauley's heavy machine gun would be too awkward to maneuver in the steep narrow gulley leading off from the one we were in. Tayo, his assistant gunner, went in first with his carbine, followed by McCauley, then me, then Flash bringing up the rear with a radio. We advanced carefully and were creeping up slowly, trying to flank the position covertly.

Suddenly McCauley whispered, "Sir, I see feet to the right! Feet to the right!"

During the long days spent in the Kuwaiti desert, I had fired hundreds of rounds through my carbine, sometimes practicing for hours on end. I had sought to build what's called "muscle memory"—training your muscles to react immediately and correctly to a given situation through intense repetition so that they will perform as a reflex no matter the level of stress.

In less than a second, I lowered the muzzle of my weapon, flexed my right knee, stepped with my left foot ninety degrees to the right, and pressed my weapon up to my cheek. My right eye was already on the sights. Through them I saw two feet, just like McCauley had said.

I didn't hesitate. I fired two shots.

After I fired the first two shots, the man sat up twelve meters directly in front of me, swinging a machine gun in our direction. I released four more rounds, sending them into his chest. McCauley opened up just after me, firing his pistol, while Tayo simultaneously shot the man in the thigh.

At that point, the man either fell back into his hole or ducked down into his position. We couldn't be sure, so we kept firing to keep his head down. I wasn't taking any chances.

It wasn't but a few seconds before Ray came tearing in from the right with Uncle Jesse on the high ground. He had been watching our movement out of the corner of his eye from fifty meters away but had mostly been worried about Sergeant Lane's team until he heard us open fire.

"Cease fire!" Ray yelled, and as I did I also grabbed McCauley's pistol to make sure he did the same.

Ray briefly halted, aimed, and fired three shots from his carbine. Then he yelled, "Clear!"

McCauley and I ran up with our weapons at the ready. There, in the hole, was the man I had shot living his last moments on Earth. After the holes I had made in his torso, Ray had shot three rounds into his head. The man was now twitching and shaking as his body went into shock. He was already dead but he was going through his death throes.

My first thought was more amazement than horror. Actions unleashed by my hand had ended the life of this man. I couldn't believe it.

My second thought is the one I never talk about. There has only been one moment in combat when I was truly frightened, and this was it.

As I looked down on the man I had just killed, I took stock of his clothes: North Face jacket, Mountain Hardware pants, and synthetic long underwear. By his clothes he looked more like a Vail ski bum than a terrorist. I then saw his weapon, an American-made M249 light machine gun.

I didn't show it to any of my men, but inside I began panicking. What if I had just killed an American soldier? Some Special Forces operator or CIA agent operating deep behind enemy lines in civilian clothes? What if the man I just shot was a friendly-fire casualty?

Ray brought me back to the moment, to the reality at hand. "Sir," he whispered patiently. "Sir, we have to get security."

I came to my senses and deployed my troops in a hasty perimeter around the body. I also told two of my soldiers to begin searching the dead man.

What they found began to put my earlier fears to rest.

Strewn among all the American equipment was a collection of Soviet-type small arms: two AK series assault rifles, three Makarov pistols, hand grenades, and Soviet ammunition. Also mixed in were assorted American gadgets usually belonging to special operations soldiers: night vision devices, load-bearing equipment vests, infrared targeting lasers, and global positioning systems. I put two and two together and realized we had discovered a cache of equipment stolen from the dead SEALs and Rangers atop Takur Ghar.

The find caused a stir. Ten minutes after the first shots were fired, Captain Rogers made his way down to the site where the dead body still lay twitching. We inventoried the equipment we had captured, and the pile at our feet began to resemble a crime scene.

I don't remember when the body stopped moving. But before we headed back out, McCauley produced a "death card" from his pocket. He had taken a deck of Kampgrounds of

171

America playing cards and written the name of our unit on each of the cards. In the Vietnam War, units would leave death cards on the enemy dead so the Viet Cong would know who had killed them. It was a form of juvenile schoolyard intimidation transplanted into a combat zone.

McCauley dropped the nine of spades onto the motionless corpse.

It read, "3rd Platoon, A Company. Jihad *this*, motherfucker."

I WISH I could say that the rest of that mission passed without incident. But as my patrol—now beefed up to two squads and a gun team—worked its way back up the gulley to the bunkers we had already hit with rockets, I watched as one of my privates, David Vasquez from Amarillo, Texas, fell to the earth and rolled away in pain as he cleared a bunker.

As the advance stalled, I called up to Ray on the radio for more information because he was closer.

"Not now!" he snapped.

Suddenly I was worried. I had known Ray to be alternately sarcastic and serious, but never flustered. I ran up the gulley to their position, to find blood everywhere, with Corporal Littrell working hard to stop the bleeding. I knew instantly that Vasquez would live, but the thought of him losing an arm while clearing a bunker that turned out to be unmanned was too much.

Vasquez had tossed the grenade into the bunker, and either the grenade hadn't gone all the way in or it had ignited something inside that had sent a spray of metal shrapnel from the darkness. Whatever the cause, I now had my first real casualty on my hands.

I kept my cool and organized a casualty evacuation, calling Captain Rogers on the radio and getting a medical treatment team to our position as soon as possible. We continued the mission, putting aside our thoughts on Vasquez's arm as we destroyed four abandoned bunkers with plastic explosives and confiscated more grenades and weapons while he was carried back to the landing zone.

THAT EVENING we also moved back to the landing zone, where we would be picked up the following morning. Colonel Matthews called us on the radio and congratulated us on the first combat action for our regiment, the 31st Infantry, since the Vietnam War. Down from our position on some high ground, I could see the brigade surgeon, flown in to treat Vasquez, working to adjust his bandages. The surgeon told me Vasquez would be fine and would fly with us back to Bagram in the morning.

Ray and I stayed up a long time that night talking. We both knew what had happened down in that valley, but we needed to talk about it. We needed to work through the details in our heads—where I was when I fired the first shots, what he thought when he heard the shots, what he saw when he crested the enemy position. Ray had killed men before, when he had been a sniper stationed in Panama. But that was a long time ago, and he had never killed anyone at close range. For me, this was my first, and although I knew that killing the enemy was my job, I had not fully come to grips with what that meant until now.

THE BIRDS SHOWED UP early the next morning. Dust kicked up into our faces until the heavy, twin-rotored Chinooks had finally settled onto the dirt and rock. We loaded up and they took us away, back to Bagram.

The view during the ride out of the valley was spectacular. I sat near the rear, where the ramp was down, and watched the Afghan mountains rise behind us as we sped away. The pilots had their fun again, swerving and swooping and bending and diving in and out of the valleys and canyons. Before long we were northward bound, heading back to Bagram. To our west we could see the decimated capital of Kabul, and farther to our west, we saw an even more amazing sight—a commercial jet landing at Kabul's new airport. Afghanistan, despite the chaos in the southeast from which I was returning, was beginning to creep back to normalcy after twenty years of anarchy.

After we got back to the base, we settled down outside our tents and cleaned our gear. Colonel Matthews dropped by, asked a few questions about my kill, shook my hand, and left. The media were hanging around the tents, asking questions of my men, and I let them. While many in the post-Vietnam military eyed the media with a wary attitude, I had come to see the reporters who told the story of what was really happening on the front lines as a positive thing. Although the modern reporter may not be as knowledgeable when it comes to the military as Vietnam-era reporters were, most are generally good people who liked talking to the soldiers. And the soldiers liked seeing their names in the newspapers, as did their families and girlfriends. Captain Rogers tried to send a few my way, but that day I wasn't in the mood to talk. Instead, I took off my jacket and began to clean my weapon while sitting on a metal air force cargo pallet.

Before long, the battalion chaplain came along and asked me if I knew where he might find Lieutenant Exum. Since the jacket with my name and rank was off, I suppose he had no way of knowing who I was, but this chaplain was a little out of touch with the men anyway. Most battalion chaplains try to know every soldier in the battalion by face, especially the officers. I was patient, though, and introduced myself.

Once my men were a few meters away, he asked if he could have a word or two with me alone. I said sure and walked over to another tent. He followed and then nervously asked if I was the lieutenant who had killed a man the day before. I told him I was. He then launched into some nonsensical stuff about how the Ten Commandments don't actually mean "Thou Shalt Not Kill" but rather "Thou Shalt Not Murder." He then took things a step further and assured me that God had wanted me to kill that man.

By this point I had stopped listening. The chaplain, for all his good intentions, was seriously undermining my faith in God, which I had previously thought to be unflappable. Hearing that man say that Jesus wanted me to be in Afghanistan ending the lives of fellow humans was too much for my faith to handle at the time. I preferred to think that what I was doing was outside of God's will, and rather one of life's ugly realities.

I thanked the chaplain, assured him that no, I wasn't having any doubts or emotional issues, and after shaking his hand walked back to my tent alone.

Over the next two days, I would dodge other chaplains sent down from Division to offer their comfort. Catching me hiding from one of them behind a stack of MREs, the company first sergeant, who was also from my hometown, laughed at me and suggested I just tell them I was a hard motherfucker from Tennessee who didn't need their counseling.

I smiled, but inwardly just wished the chaplains would go away.

I FELT SORRY for the chaplains, and today often think about something Colonel Matthews said to me a few days after we returned from that mission. He told me that while most folks in the outside world—and even many in the army—*think* they know what we do for a living, very few *really* understand. They can't relate to the people who actually pull the triggers, the people who actually end the lives of other men. It's a lesson I have never forgotten when I talk about my experiences as a soldier. People I don't know very well or am meeting for the first time often blurt out the first thing on their minds when they learn I have been in combat.

"Did you kill anyone?" they ask.

Amazing.

I usually answer yes, and watch as things get real quiet.

After that, most people I meet are humbled and silenced

by the weight of the one-word answer that they are now trying to process in their heads. Unless they're really obnoxious, they usually don't ask any more questions about it.

It's odd that at a time when so many of my soldiers found the Bible and Christianity to be a balm, I found them repulsive. I have always been religious, but as I explained to a pastor back home after my return from Afghanistan, when I'm in combat, I try to shut out my faith. It's almost as if I can't do my job the way I know it needs to be done and be a Christian at the same time. My job in that valley was a dark task, if not an evil one. I guess I don't want to stain my faith by allowing the two worlds to meet.

When I'm on a bird going into a combat mission, I have two rituals. First, I tie a piece of green string around my right wrist and don't take it off until I've returned. At home today, these green strings hang on a hook in my bathroom, a reminder of places I have been and the job I do.

Second, I close my eyes and say a prayer. When I open my eyes, I'm a different person. I'm colder, quieter, more focused. I don't talk to God again until I'm on the bird home. Remembering the man I was while on a mission, I'm more than a little scared by him. I fear that one day I'll open my eyes to become that cold man and won't be able to return.

In *Unforgiven*, Clint Eastwood's character observes that it's a hard thing to kill a man. You take away everything he's got and everything he'll ever have. But he leaves out the part where you lose something yourself. I believe you give up your soul, one piece at a time. My Presbyterian guilt doesn't allow me to consider that I somehow won't be held responsible for what I have done when I stand before the Almighty one day.

That night after we returned from the mission, I stayed up and read by flashlight. One of the books I brought with me to Kuwait and then Afghanistan was a volume by the Argentinean writer Jorge Luis Borges. In it, he writes, "Whosoever would undertake some atrocious enterprise should act as if it were already accomplished, should impose upon himself a future as irrevocable as the past."

I resolved to view my own acts as inevitable. That man, I reasoned, was dead long before I stepped foot into the valley, and I was a killer long before I pumped four rounds into his torso.

I wrote a letter to the English professor at Penn who'd introduced me to Borges two years before, then turned off my flashlight.

I slept easily that night.

XII

We had one more mission to accomplish before we could head home. The Shah-e-Kot Valley, which we had cleared of enemy fighters in the previous missions, was still littered with enemy positions and equipment. Our mission was to ride in on helicopters with two platoons—mine and Greg's—and work our way through the valley with a Green Beret team and some Afghan natives, blowing up everything we came across along the way.

The night before we left, I went to see Vasquez in the medical tent before they evacuated him to Oman and then on to Germany for surgery. He was heavily sedated. The plan was for General Franklin "Buster" Hagenbeck himself to come down to pin the Purple Heart onto Vasquez in the presence of the battalion's officers and the sergeants from my platoon. I knelt by Vasquez's bed, explaining to him what was going to happen, unsure of how much of it registered with him.

Vasquez had joined the platoon while we were in Kuwait, as much a physical mess as other young privates were physical specimens. One of them, a seventeen-year-old from Detroit named Butts had been through Michigan's juvenile correctional "Scared Straight" Boot Camp not once but twice and had come to the platoon fitter and stronger than most of the sergeants. Vasquez on the other hand could barely do twenty push-ups when he first joined us and struggled to stay in formation during runs. When I asked him if he had played any sports in high school, he replied that he had been a member of the academic decathlon team. Apparently he traveled to high schools around Texas and competed in math quizzes while his peers played football.

As such, Vasquez—or "Fat-quez" as Sergeant Lane initially called him—came in for a lot of abuse at first. But he soon endeared himself to us. He was quick-witted and possessed an awesome recall of the same old songs Ray and I quizzed Flash on to no avail. As out of shape as Vasquez was when he arrived, he also came with an abundance of good humor and wit. Physically, he never became a stud like Butts, but he adapted to the physical rigor of the job and conditioned himself to at least keep up with the rest of the platoon.

After thirty minutes of waiting, the word came down that the general couldn't come before Vasquez left. I broke the news to Vasquez, who replied in a drugged voice that he understood, that the general was an old man. At that point I cut him off and we all laughed at what else Vasquez might say about the general while under the influence of drugs if we let him. I patted Vasquez on the shoulder and left him to get some rest.

The next morning, we landed near the town of Marzak in the south of the valley. The Whale was to our northwest and the area where we had killed the machine gunner was nearby to the east. As hard as it was to believe, this place had been a desperate battleground just a few weeks earlier. Now allied Afghan forces occupied lookout positions on all the hills surrounding the town and the area was almost completely free of the hundreds of al-Qaeda fighters who had populated the valley a month earlier.

We landed on a farmer's field that lay fallow and unplanted. The fields in the valley were on steppes, with small rock walls separating the individual plots of land. The rock walls made it easy for Greg and me to set up a defensive perimeter for the night. We were guarding not so much against the enemy that first night as we were against looters. I wondered if we would catch an Afghan trying to sneak into the perimeter to steal a piece of equipment from someone.

For this mission, I had plenty of extra players in the platoon, including two explosives experts and a dog handler. The explosives experts would no doubt be useful. But I had no idea what I was going to do with the dog handler and his German shepherd, Joop, who lay dozing a few feet from my rucksack. We had to leave our other platoon back at Bagram to accommodate all the extra personnel.

In the morning, we moved out through what had been the scene of dozens of American casualties, a tight mountain pass first named Objective Ginger and later christened the Ginger Pass. Two rifle companies from the Tenth Mountain Division had tried to land here and establish a blocking position during Anaconda. But after the assault by indigenous Afghan forces fell apart, the al-Qaeda mortarmen were able to devote all their time and ammunition to dropping rounds on the American soldiers in the pass. The Americans were chewed up and had to be evacuated in the night.

We stepped over the boulders, trying to keep our balance, the entrance to the Upper Shah-e-Kot just ahead of us and marked by a burned-out antiaircraft gun. We cleared the valley as we walked, putting tape around the land mines we discovered and stopping whenever we found a large ammunition cache or a bunker for demolition.

About three hundred meters into the valley, we found a series of small caves and bunkers in a gulley to the left. The valley ran from west to east, and the gulley ran up to the north about two hundred meters, growing steeper and steeper the farther you went. We climbed up and into the bunkers, where we found hundreds of rockets and boxes of ammunition stacked four feet high in places. Mujahideen and, later, the Taliban, had been stocking this valley with supplies for decades, preparing to hold this area against foreign invaders until the bitter end. They had held the Russians and the tribal factions that followed. But the Americans had driven them out of their fortress. Now my platoon stood in their reinforced positions as we strung detonation cord through them and placed plastic explosives on all the rockets.

I was about to pull the fuse igniter on this giant arms cache when an Afghan tribesman came running up to me with a pleading smile on his face. The Green Beret with us explained that before we destroyed everything the tribesman wanted to

THIS MAN'S ARMY

salvage the bags of Taliban grain and rice from the cave for his men. That was fine by me, of course, and a group of eight cheerful militiamen snaked up the gulley to the cave at the top and disappeared inside.

When they emerged, they all had heavy bags of rice on their shoulders and began to walk back down. Their leader, the man who had appealed to me to wait for them to salvage the grain, came out of the cave with his AK-47 slung over his shoulder and a teapot in his hands. He presented his gift to me with great fanfare and gratitude, doing his best to communicate that the teapot had belonged to the fighters in the cave and that he was giving it to me for allowing his soldiers to take the grain.

"Al-Qaeda!" he said to me as he pressed the teapot into my chest.

I smiled and said, "Yes, al-Qaeda."

"Al-Qaeda!" he said again, waving good-bye and bounding down the steep gulley with his smile still plastered to his face.

One of the Afghanis was obviously the joker in their little band and smiled and laughed with my men, slapping them on the back and showing off his AK-47, which he had decorated with colored beads and bright tape. He was fascinated by Flash, having probably never seen an Asian-American. The Afghanis vaguely understood that Americans came in both black and white colors, but to him Flash was an oddity. The joker pointed at him, struggled to find the words, and finally yelled, "Japanese! Yes!"

I shook my head, laughing as Flash stood there with an awkward, embarrassed smile on his face. I wondered how I

183

was going to explain Flash, the American son of Chinese immigrants from Vietnam. It seemed too many nationalities to sort out.

I just smiled and said, "No, no. Chinese."

This delighted the joker, who threw back his head and yelled, "Ah, yes. Yes! China. China!"

From then on, the Afghanis singled Flash out, yelling "China!" whenever they saw him. He became a talisman for them, and they always smiled when they saw him. We echoed back "China!" in response, a fraternal connection between two groups of soldiers who had no idea how to communicate otherwise.

As for Flash, we all had a good laugh at his expense that day, and to my knowledge folks in the company still point at him on occasion and yell "China!" with a laugh.

I finally pulled the plug on the explosives, hurrying down the gulley to safety. We had laid them out on top of the ammunition and rockets, hoping to push the explosion downward, sending the rockets exploding onto themselves. I waited for the explosions, and they arrived in grand form, sending dirt and small rocks high into the air and crashing back down on us four hundred meters away and over a ridge. We hugged the walls of the valley until the rocks stopped falling. Someone said "Jesus" in awe.

The explosions continued. Smaller, higher pitched. Secondary explosions following the two big ones.

The next cache was less than a hundred meters further into the valley. A huge stack of recoilless rifle rounds—rockets really—lay piled on one another in a corner where the boulders had formed a little covered bed. I ordered the platoon to begin stacking the rockets, and then ordered Butts to start counting them. Ray and I laughed at Butts counting aloud, and shouted out random numbers—56! 247! 84!—to confuse him. Butts arrived at the number 486, and I made him count again. Once again, 486. When stacked, the pile of rockets stood four feet high and spread out thirty feet. I told Flash to take a picture. I wanted to remember such a ridiculously large cache.

At that point, Captain Rogers radioed to tell me that we had to go back and clear a path through the valley so that Bobby Whitesocks and the Humvees with our rucksacks could make their way through. Two land mines lay at the bottom of the gulley in which we had just set the charges, and they blocked the path any vehicles would take. I ordered Ray to stay behind and to set the charges on the rockets with the help of the demolitions experts while I walked back with Sergeant Wallace's squad to see what we could do about the mines.

When I got back to the gulley, the caches that we had previously exploded were now on fire, and the ammunition was burning. I stood with Third Squad behind a boulder, watching rockets and bullets catch fire and fly into the southern wall of the valley. To get to the mines as well as a smaller ammo cache we had not destroyed, we would have to cross through those flying bullets and rockets. I looked behind me at the nervous soldiers who waited to see what I would decide.

I radioed back to Sergeant Montoya, telling him that while I would send myself into that crossfire to blow up those mines, I didn't feel comfortable asking anyone else to run such a risk, least of all Padilla, the combat engineer attached to our platoon. No sooner had I said that than Ray interjected on the radio.

"That's bullshit! I'm coming down there myself."

Ray had previously been a combat engineer and had told us all about all the dangerous things he had done—stupid things really, like lying down only ten meters from a bangalore torpedo before exploding it. The minimum safe distance for a bangalore torpedo was three hundred meters. But at that moment I needed someone else to help me blow up the mines and that cache, another "brave" (read: "stupid") man, not just me.

Ray arrived and demanded to see where the cache and mines were. Just then a .50-caliber bullet flew over our heads, sounding like an angry hornet and followed shortly by the crash of a rocket into the south wall, which sent up a plume of smoke and dust.

"Shit," Ray admitted with a grin as he surveyed the explosions ahead.

With that nervous smirk still on his face, he asked me how I wanted to do this. I could tell that he had just come to grips with the danger of what we were about to do but had decided to do it anyway. This was either because he really was brave or because he had decided he had talked too much shit to back down now.

We split the demolitions up between the two of us. I took two blocks of C4 to destroy the mines, which lay sixty meters away and in the direct line of fire from the bullets that continued to spit from the caches. Ray took a few more blocks of C4, and we put it all in small bags that we slung around our necks. Then, with a deep breath and a knowing look across at one another, we ran off into the mouth of the gulley. I heard a few bullets whiz above my head before I reached relative safety behind a boulder next to the mines. I looked back to where Ray had found the cache as he also sought shelter behind some rocks.

Another rocket flew above us and crashed into the wall to our south. We were laughing now in spite of ourselves, giddy with fear, scared out of our minds and full of gallows humor. Ray shouted over the din that "the specter of death is certainly hovering over us now," borrowing a favorite line from Captain Rogers.

I pulled the C4 out of my bag, tying detonation cord around the blocks. Then gently, ever so gently, I placed them on top of the mines. I waited until Ray was done, feeling my heart skip a few beats every time a rocket exploded. I was about a foot away from the closest of the land mines, now rigged for demolition, and every time I heard an explosion I imagined it was the land mine exploding prematurely. This was nerve-racking stuff.

Ray was finally done. I looked over at him, and we pulled the pins on out of the detonators at the same time. We had about five minutes to run to safety, which was plenty of time given the speed with which I ran out of that gulley, comically trying to duck the flying bullets along the way—as if we could even do such a thing as dodge a bullet, *Matrix*-style.

We had slowed to a walk by the time we heard the land mines and the cache go off. I paused to catch my breath. I tried to understand what had led Ray and me to dart into that draw, risking our lives to destroy two land mines and a few boxes of ammunition. It was a kind of macho one-upmanship, yes, but also something else. I tried to place the source of that type of misguided courage, that laughter in the face of danger, but I was at a loss to do so.

After a few more hours, the secondary explosions would die down and the Humvees would be able to make it past the gulley and to us. But first we had to detonate that pile of 486 rockets. The demo experts had placed a line of blocks of C4 across the top of the rockets, creating a "ribbon charge." We retreated to a safe distance before that charge went off. We had plugged our ears but could hear the massive explosion anyway and felt the thud rattle in our chests.

I took a team and walked back to where the pile of rockets had been. Not a thing remained. There was nothing left at all. Unlike the previous blast, which set off those dangerous secondary explosions, this one was clean. Nothing remained except for a large black scar on the ground. You could tell how massive the blast was, though. Forty meters up the walls of the valley, a solitary tree burned from the fire.

We walked back to where the rest of the platoon was, pausing just long enough for Greg's platoon to blow up a pile of mortar rounds. We had now reached the spot in the valley where we had shot the al-Qaeda machine gunner and Vasquez—by now evacuated to Germany—had been wounded. As we walked by the turn to the dead al-Qaeda fighter, we all found ourselves looking toward the scene from a few days earlier.

Captain Rogers was far ahead with Greg's platoon. I couldn't reach him on the radio, but I succeeded in reaching his radio operator and asked for permission to push forward and clear the southern fork in the valley where no one had been yet. Earlier, Captain Rogers had told me to wait and not to proceed any farther, but I was bored now and wanted to push on ahead. The radio operator also couldn't reach the captain, so I informed him I was moving my platoon forward. Captain Rogers was surprised when he learned from his radio operator that I had pushed forward, but the most he chastised me that night was with a smile and a shake of the head. He admired my aggressive and naturally insubordinate nature because he shared it—it was what had gotten us into Afghanistan in the first place.

We had gone about four hundred meters up into the valley when we made the biggest find yet. In three separate caches, we found more than 500 mortar rounds, more than 250 rocket-propelled grenades, almost 100 more recoilless rocket rounds, boxes of land mines, boxes of ammunition, and an unexploded twenty-five-hundred-pound USAF bomb right in the middle of the three caches. For the next two hours, we set explosives on the three caches. Ray had the idea to link all the caches together with detonation cord so when we blew them up, they would all explode together. If we tried to explode all the caches separately, they might set off the others nearby and ignite lots of secondary explosions that could block off the valley for days. But to explode all the caches at the same time, we needed lots more C4 and det cord. The two Green Berets with us were more than happy to oblige, driving their ATVs back to their camp for more C4. The Green Beret commander later told Captain Rogers that he was impressed with how much we all knew about demolitions, but he should have expected it given how much C4 we had been using since we arrived in the country.

We split into teams for the big caches. Ray and I handled the mortar cache where the bulk of the munitions were, stacking everything with Flash's help and laying out a ribbon charge over all the rounds. The demo experts set the charge on the other caches. All together, we used two and half cases of C4 and three spools of detonation cord to set up all the charges. As a coup de grâce, I stuffed a block of C4 into the air force bomb and linked it up with the other charges.

By the time we retreated to a safe distance, it was nearing sundown. Greg's platoon was crowing about how big their last explosion had been, and we told them to just wait—and to put their heads down—for the explosion we were about to set off. Everyone got behind rocks and prepared for the blast. The valley was dark by now, the sun having set already to the west and the last moments of light playing themselves out in the dusk twilight.

When the explosion went off, I remember the valley turning bright with light for two or three seconds. The blast provided us all with one last burst of light, and then we heard the booming explosions that pounded our eardrums, despite our earplugs. Someone yelled "Incoming," and in one of the scariest moments of the whole war, we could hear some giant piece of metal or rock spinning in the air above us, *whoomp, whoomp, whoomp,* deep and frightening.

Soon whatever went flying through the air—we later reckoned it to be a piece of the air force bomb—landed and we all stood up. There, before us, was a giant mushroom cloud about six hundred meters ahead. It rose huge and black against the dark blue sky, and we all stared at it, awestruck, as the secondary explosions that would continue through the night began to go off.

That night we lay down to sleep in a tight perimeter. Greg's platoon took the south half of the clock face and my platoon took the north. We occasionally heard the *pop pop pop* of the remaining bullets among the detonated ordnance heating up and catching fire, and to the east where our massive charges went off, we could see a faint glow where some trees had caught fire.

I lay on a bed of pine needles and crushed cardboard MRE boxes that night, trying to stay warm enough under my poncho liner to get some sleep. I thought about what a stupid thing it had been for Ray and I to run into that gulley and detonate those mines. We should have been more cautious and waited. We knew this was our last mission in Afghanistan, and there was no need to take such extreme risks. But there we were, running, laughing from the fear, playing with plastic explosives as the bullets whizzed overhead.

I thought of Dienekes the Spartan at Thermopylae, laughing that the massive salvos of fearsome Medean arrows would be "all the better—we will fight in the shade." After I got back to America and received a letter from one of my old classics professors in college thanking me for my service and congratulating me on my safe return, I wrote back and thanked him right back, telling him that the Greeks taught me, among other things, how to be brave.

WE AWAKENED at dawn. Greg's platoon stayed behind to take care of some caches they had not been able to destroy the day before. My platoon headed back to the eastern half of the valley, toward areas that had not yet been seen by American forces. Ray's squad and the Green Beret team leader crawled through a particularly tight section of the valley through which al-Qaeda forces had no doubt fled after the battle turned sour for them.

The farther east we went, the fewer fortified positions and caches we found. We had pushed beyond the al-Qaeda strongpoints, and all we had left to clear or destroy was one last complex consisting of about nine bunkers, which we searched individually, grabbing all the documents we could find before setting C4 in the support rafters that held the bunkers up. It took all day. When we could, we just blew the bunkers up with "bunker buster" rockets and left them. There were dead bodies in and around them. In one mortar position, which had obviously been struck by the air force, two dead al-Qaeda fighters lay amid splintered wood and disarray, their open wounds filled with maggots. The stench was unbearable. No one in the platoon wanted to search the bodies. I certainly wouldn't, and I wouldn't make anyone else do it. We radioed for soldiers from the criminal investigation detachment with Captain Rogers to come forward, and they arrived to take DNA samples and search the bodies while wearing rubber gloves.

In some ways, the valley was one large crime scene. No one could be sure whether or not any of the dead fighters were terrorists accused of previous attacks, so the CID guys took DNA samples off everyone.

Most of the bunkers in the last stretch we discovered were built in a gulley much like the one in which we had killed the machine gunner on the previous mission. It was clear that the fighters in the valley had been well organized. One bunker had been reserved entirely for medical supplies. Another bunker was a library of sorts, with all sorts of manuals and books written in Arabic. Yet another bunker was a kitchen. The stovepipe that pushed up through the roof was tied to a tree so that when the smoke rose, the tree, which gave off its own heat signature, would mask the heat and confuse American thermal scanners in the sky.

These al-Qaeda were smart fuckers, we thought to ourselves.

Toward the top of the gulley, we found a cave about fifty meters deep. I went in about twenty meters and came out when I couldn't see the entrance anymore. Night vision goggles aren't very useful in deep caves because of the lack of ambient light. I marked the cave and went back to destroying the bunkers with our explosives and our shoulder-launched rockets.

I worked my way through the bunkers, tying off blocks of C4 and stuffing them into the roofs of the caves while Flash gave me cover with his carbine. I taught other guys how to tie the C4 blocks the proper way, and they began to help. Since the intelligence guys with us had already looked through the library bunker and taken what they wanted, I looked the other way as men put stuff into their packs to send home, books written in Arabic and other harmless trinkets.

The Afghanis arrived to clear the cave we had found. They desperately wanted to put themselves in harm's way before us, which was warming in a way and made us feel appreciated. They were grateful to us for helping them defeat the Taliban, and at the same time, the canny Afghanis were aware how much we avoided casualties and understood our political realties back home, that support for the war was directly tied to how painless it was in terms of American losses.

Earlier in the war, the Green Berets who fought alongside the allied warlords and directed air strikes had been carefully shielded from as much danger as possible by the warlords, who feared that if too many Americans died, the U.S. government and generals would call the American soldiers home and the warlords would once again be left to fight the Taliban alone. Americans may debate whether or not an American life is worth more than a foreigner's. That's a luxury we enjoy. But for the Afghanis, the answer to that question was clear: American lives were undoubtedly worth more.

As we waited for them to clear the cave, we found what was probably a dead Chechen in the mouth of the gulley. The intelligence we had said we could tell the Chechens by their Asiatic features.

"He look Asian to you, Flash?" I asked.

Flash stared at the man and shrugged.

This guy looked Asian, I guess, but mostly he looked dead. His eyes had been eaten out by maggots long ago, and his face was bruised and burned. The al-Qaeda took great care to bury most of their dead or carry them off, but I guess they had been in a hurry to leave the valley and this guy wasn't important enough to take care of.

After a long afternoon spent blowing up bunkers and marking that cave, we left the valley and walked back the two kilometers to where the helicopters had dropped us off in the middle of the farm's fields. On the way back, we destroyed a bunker for the benefit of Colonel Matthews, who wanted to watch us use our new bunker buster rockets. We fired the rocket from closer than we should have, and the resulting explosion sent rocks flying back at us. His staff dove for cover, but Colonel Matthews sat there on one knee beside me, refusing to even shield his face. While I sat there embarassed, he just laughed and teased me about putting him in harm's way.

All the soldiers loved our battalion commander. He exuded confidence and a warrior spirit despite his thin frame and lean profile. Half-Afghani himself, he had been adopted as a child by a U.S. Army sergeant from his biological mother, a German, and raised in Georgia as a naturalized citizen. On the way out, he insisted that we stop by where we had killed that al-Qaeda a week earlier. We walked up to where the engagement took place, and Ray and I described what had happened. The body of the man I shot still lay there, covered by the blanket that Corporal Littrell had placed over him but now stinking something awful.

We slowly patrolled back to the landing zone. Walking point, at the front of the platoon, was Specialist Causey, a soldier who had arrived in my platoon after some minor disciplinary problems in another battalion at Fort Drum. Since he had arrived with our platoon, however, he had been a model soldier. Just a few weeks earlier, while we were in Kuwait, his wife had given birth to a daughter. Causey was getting out of the army upon our return, and I can only imagine he was praying that nothing would happen here in Afghanistan that would prevent him from returning home safe and sound. He already had a job lined up and a family waiting on him, but as was typical of so many soldiers in my platoon, he never complained about serving in Afghanistan, or risking his life by walking point at the lead of the platoon. If we crossed a land mine, or were ambushed, he would likely be the first one killed. I turned around and told Flash that guys like Causey are what makes America great—men that would risk everything for their country even though they have plenty to lose.

After we arrived back at the farm, we reestablished the perimeter we had set two nights earlier. We were all exhausted and immediately fell asleep. Even the guards had trouble staying awake, and the squad leaders made rounds throughout the night to make sure they were awake and protecting the perimeter from thieves.

In the middle of the night, I was awakened and told that a column of about a hundred al-Qaeda was advancing on a small team of Green Berets twenty miles to the north. It looked like we might get called upon to march all night and engage the enemy forces.

I told the squad leaders, and Ray and I laughed with excitement, joking that this was surely the greatest war ever, one in which you spent all day blowing things up and then set out in the night to go kill a bunch of bad guys with the help of the Air Force. For us, while we were on the missions, all of this was an adventure. Putting all the reservations we felt toward killing aside, this was one big game, a game in which we were winning by a landslide against an overmatched opponent.

But the threat subsided, we were never called, and the next morning we boarded helicopters and finally left the Shah-e-Kot Valley. On the way out, I was once again toward the rear of the helicopter, to watch as the floor of the valley rushed below us and faded from view for the last time.

The crew chief had a wild look in his eye and moved past

me as he held on to a small tether and leaned out the back of the helicopter. Soon he crawled over to me and asked above the din of the chopper, "Hey, sir! You got any grenades?"

"Sure," I yelled, "we all got grenades."

"Throw one out the back!" he yelled with a mischievous grin on his face.

"You're fucking crazy," I told him.

"No, no," he said. "It's cool! The pilots say it's okay."

I looked back at Captain Rogers. He shrugged.

Soon I was standing on the rear ramp of the CH-47 Chinook with a grenade in my hand, the pin pulled. Captain Rogers stood up behind me and grabbed on to the back of my body armor to make sure I didn't fall out.

"You better make a good fucking throw or we're all toast," he helpfully reminded me.

When the crew chief gave me the thumbs-up to indicate there weren't any civilians below, I heaved the grenade out the back. The platoon watched it land, sit for a moment as we sped away, and then send up a plume of smoke upon exploding. The helicopter erupted in cheers, and several soldiers who had taken a picture of my infamous toss told me they planned on using the photo to blackmail me in the future. I just laughed and settled back onto my rucksack. I would be famous within the company for months to come as "that crazy fuck who threw the grenade out of the helicopter."

We landed back at Bagram around lunchtime, filled with relief that—barring some emergency—our combat missions were over.

During the mission in which my platoon killed the al-Qaeda soldier, we had two reporters in the rear of our patrol, and they witnessed the aftermath of our assault. After we returned from that mission, the higher-ranking officers and sergeants major fretted over what the reporters might write in their stories. They worried that the reporters might not understand what we had done, why we had fired so many bullets, and what my soldiers had done after the man was dead, when Corporal Littrell cut the clothes off the body with a knife to search him. We had not done anything wrong or even inconsistent with army doctrine, so I was angered when I heard that some officers wanted to question us about what we had done.

But that was nowhere near as angry as I was when I was awakened at midnight one night and told to report to the mess tent along with the soldiers involved in the shooting. The major conducting the investigation could tell I wasn't happy when I walked in with my sleepy soldiers following me. The seven of us sat down, were told to complete sworn statements about what happened, and were then told that all of this was just a precaution. One of the reporters worked for a national magazine, and the officers weren't sure how he would interpret our actions. In case the reporter's story branded us as anything less than heroic, the officers just wanted to have our statements on record for use in a rebuttal.

It was complete bullshit. If the reporter's story was negative, the officers could use our statements as proof that the army had already taken action and was on its way toward prosecuting the offenders. With our sworn statements, they could put together an investigation to find us guilty of "excessive violence" or something equally ridiculous.

Whoever heard of excessive violence in a war? How could a general who dropped ten-thousand-pound bombs on enemy soldiers accuse McCauley and me of being excessive because we had fired half a magazine of ammo at an enemy soldier? The al-Qaeda soldier was above us in a dug-in fighting position—most of the bullets we fired had hit the dirt in front of him, not the fighter himself.

We had done nothing wrong, and as they covered their asses collecting our sworn statements, they assured us of that.

"Oh yes, we understand," they told us. "This is just a formality."

Since the military rejected the draft after the Vietnam War, the army has become more professional and, by proxy, less amateur. The effects have been mostly for the better: officers are better educated, make a more serious study of tactics, and commit themselves to service for the long haul. But the system has worked out for the worse in some cases. Increasingly, being an officer in the army is no longer a temporary service to the country—it's a career. Consequently, officers are often looking out for their own futures rather than for the safety and good of their men. In Afghanistan, the army brass saw the media coverage as one of the biggest dangers to their careers. With media given a much broader ability to report the war than they had in the first Persian Gulf war, the brass worried how they and their men (but mostly they) would be portrayed in the news back home and abroad.

Still, there are plenty of great career officers out there. One of them, Captain Rogers, was waiting for me when I walked back to the tent that night, and it was tough to tell who was angrier about the investigation, he or I.

It turned out the brass had nothing to worry about. The article that was published the following week was glowing.

The reporter portrayed my platoon and me as heroes. There wasn't even any mention of us firing too many bullets or the fact that Corporal Littrell cut off the man's jacket and shirt with his knife as he searched him.

Overall, I can't complain too much about the officers I've met in the army, even the staff officers I hated so much in Kuwait. Most of them have been abnormally decent people, men who could have been making more money elsewhere but had elected to serve their country in anonymity instead. My battalion commander, Colonel Matthews—the best officer I have ever served with, including my time in the Rangers— always told me how lucky he felt to be working with so many talented men, all dedicated to their country. For every incompetent or bitter officer there were four who desired only to serve America, and they served it well.

XIII

NOTHING PREPARED ME for the inevitable return home. The company was weary as opposed to jubilant that day we boarded the C-17 cargo jet out of Bagram en route to Uzbekistan and then Germany, where we disembarked and boarded a commercial jet for the final leg home to Fort Drum.

Home was, for me, a relative concept. It wasn't as if I would have any friends to greet me or throw their arms around me in upstate New York, so I couldn't really consider that home. The only people I knew there were the men I had been with for the past seven months. But all the same, I was looking forward to drinking a beer and spending time alone for the first time since October.

But first we arrived in Germany, at an airbase south of Frankfurt, bleary-eyed, at two in the morning. Our flight to the U.S. didn't leave until noon the next day. I had the presence of mind to find out when last call at the All Ranks' Club was, and upon learning it wasn't for another hour, I led the collective charge for beer. None of us had really drank for the better part of the past year—I'd only had my Christmas scotch, a few nips of black market vodka in Afghanistan, and a shot of Jim Beam a CNN cameraman sneaked me. After one pitcher that night, I was drunk already, but I dimly remember drinking more with guys from the platoon, until the sun began to creep up over the outlines of our temporary barracks. I also remember laughing, telling stories, losing to Junk in video games in the club until they kicked us out around four, and subsequently liberating several bottles of beer from a room in which some air force guys were sleeping.

After a full thirty minutes of sleep and with both of us still quite drunk, Sergeant Lane woke me up around seven, in time for breakfast. We helped each other into the dining hall and sat, exhausted and queasy, staring at our scrambled eggs and sipping water and juice in an effort to head off the inevitable hangovers we would soon be facing. My men told me over breakfast that aside from Greg, who didn't drink, I was the only officer who had survived the night without puking. I took some pride in that, despite the fact that I was now busily ingesting Tylenol and carrying a water bottle with me as I stumbled around the airbase.

One of my soldiers' wives was from Germany, and she had driven to the base to see her husband the night before. She offered to show a few of us around Frankfurt that morning in her car, and though I was both terribly hungover—as well as worried we might somehow miss our flight—I accepted her offer. Our tour took about an hour, and as we passed a pub in the middle of the city around nine in the morning, the eighteen-year-old private next to me asked me if I thought we could get a beer there this early. I couldn't think of anything I wanted less.

We made it back to the base with plenty of time and assembled in the terminal to board our plane. While we were gone, the first sergeant had paid off the air force guys whose beer we had stolen. They were threatening to call the MPs. Now the company was hanging out in the terminal reading and sleeping off hangovers.

When we had stopped in Uzbekistan, one of the sergeants and I had sprinted to the PX there and bought all the magazines and newspapers we could lay our hands on. The men in my company were sitting in the plush seats while they readied the airplane, reading the magazines we had grabbed and gawking at the new *Army Times*, which featured a story about my platoon's action in the Shah-e-Kot Valley and had a picture of Flash on the cover with the words DEADLY FIND. The article went on to describe how McCauley and I had killed the al-Qaeda soldier.

The sergeant major of the other battalion with us, a giant bear of a man who was the senior enlisted soldier present, was one of those no-nonsense soldiers one hopes will always be in the army, no matter how politically correct or sanitized the services become. Wounded in the first few hours of Operation Anaconda, he had described the scene of chaos on the ground to a *Time* magazine reporter after he returned to Bagram and was treated: "My men were whacking people. I'm talking nose-to-nose. I saw one man get knocked down by two AK rounds to the chest, get up, and return fire. We put the capital M in Miracle."

Reading those words in *Time*, it was tough not to be inspired.

Now he shouted above the din of conversing soldiers as we began to check the flight manifests.

"Listen up, fucksticks!"

He then ran down the list of soldiers who were supposed to board. The sergeant major led us onto the plane, a 767 chartered by the military to ferry us home. Only this plane belonged to one of the quasi-public airlines owned by the government, and unlike the kind and enthusiastic stewardesses on the Delta flight on the way to Kuwait, these stewards were male and rude, reminding us that if we acted up we could get prosecuted under the Uniform Code of Military Justice. My question was, who the fuck were these guys, and couldn't they see that we were just anxious to get home? We had been deployed for seven months, and the last thing any of my men wanted to hear was some flamboyantly effeminate steward talk down to them and threaten them with jail if they misbehaved.

The flight passed without incident, however, and we landed at Fort Drum to chilly temperatures and minimal fanfare. All the wives and families were waiting for us back at the barracks, so only the senior officers of the division were at the airfield to shake our hands. We finally made our way through customs inspections, got on some buses, and drove to the barracks, where there were pizzas and cold beer waiting.

Stepping into my office at Fort Drum for the first time in so long was like stepping into a time capsule. I had changed so much since I left that office that walking back inside was like reading a page of my personal history preserved for safe-keeping. The *New York Post* photograph of Osama bin Laden I had tacked to the wall was still there, along with the bullet hole McCauley had added to his forehead in pencil. So too were the red fleece and khakis I had worn into work the day before we left. Taking my desert fatigues off and putting those civilian clothes back on was like shedding a layer of skin and crawling into something foreign, something that didn't quite feel right yet.

After hugging Sergeant Montoya's wife and kids, returning my weapons to the arms room, and warning the boys from the platoon not to get into any trouble on their first night back in the States, I went to retrieve my car from the long-term parking lot on the other side of post. My car had a flat tire and wouldn't start, so I spent thirty minutes charging the battery and pumping more air into the tire before I could go anywhere. The third platoon leader in the company, the one I didn't care for, helped me inflate my tire. It was now April, but after nightfall, and the air at Fort Drum was still cold enough to freeze your breath. As we worked together in the cold, I regretted having been so curt with him over the course of the deployment.

As I drove off post and back to my apartment, I felt strange. I can't describe what it was like to drive onto American highways and roads again, seeing McDonald's and farmhouses and billboards. I drove on in the dark, heading west along NY Route 3 to Sackets Harbor.

I always told my men and the people who wrote me while I was deployed that I was glad I didn't have a girlfriend or wife waiting for me back home. It would have tortured me to think of someone sitting helplessly back in the United States while I was abroad risking my life. It was far better, I felt, that I was a single guy with no attachments.

But I had also known that this moment would arrive, when I would walk into my messy apartment layered with seven months of dust. Four cans of aged Pabst Blue Ribbon in the fridge were about the most inviting things there that first night back. I thought of the married men in the company and those with girlfriends, how they were spending time with them, being affectionate, feeling the embrace of a real live woman after so long a time spent in the company of men. As much as I had been looking forward to spending some time alone, I soon remembered that loneliness isn't all it's cracked up to be.

The next day I woke up late and wandered down the street to a restaurant to get something to eat. I have told friends that the weirdest sensation I have felt since I returned was as I walked down the sidewalk that first day, in civilian clothes and without a weapon. As I sat down at the bar, I instinctively slid back on the stool to allow for the carbine that had rested across my chest at every meal for the past few weeks. At that moment, I felt like an amputee feeling for his ghost leg.

I was similarly taken aback when I ordered a beer with my meal and then opened my wallet afterward to pay for it. American capitalism was going to take some getting used to. For the next few weeks, I kept thinking that I was spending an awful amount of money. I hadn't realized what a conspicuous consumer I was, but then, I had just returned from an environment in which I didn't have to pay for anything, much less the day-to-day necessities like gas, milk, and food.

If walking around without a weapon was the biggest adjustment, the second biggest shock came when I visited the mall in Watertown. As I walked the mall, I felt like a stranger in my own country. To anyone else there that day, I'm sure I looked quite normal, just another white guy in khakis, wearing a white T-shirt, black jacket, and a baseball cap. I could have been any other man in the mall. But I felt that I also should have been wearing some sort of cardboard sign that read "War Veteran" or "Be nice to me. I have just returned from Afghanistan." When the kid at the movie theater box office made me wait for five minutes while he talked on the phone, I wanted to rip his trachea out.

Americans—like citizens in most democracies—don't regard their soldiers or veterans with too much awe. We occasionally hold patriotic rallies and send cards and cookies to troops overseas, but soldiers largely live outside the mainstream culture and are outsiders, even though they often look just like everyone else. Even during the patriotic swell that accompanied Gulf War II, for example, Republicans controlling Congress and the White House moved to slash veterans' benefits. For my part, I began to fall victim to the most common sin among soldiers, the sin of self-righteousness. I genuinely felt that society—those people in the mall, those people at the bar—ought to treat me with deference.

My mother came up the next weekend to visit. I think she felt the need to physically inspect me, to make sure there really weren't any bullet holes or scars. This might be a common reaction for a member of the Vietnam generation. Having seen so many of her friends return from Vietnam broken and wounded, maybe she refused to believe I wasn't as well.

But more likely, I think she was just being a mother. I may grow older and go off to fight in wars and lead men into battle, but she figures she'll always be my mom.

A week after we returned, while my mother was still visiting, Fort Drum hosted a big welcome home ceremony for us. The Secretary of the Army was there, in addition to the Corps commander, a three-star general. Both of New York's senators, Hillary Clinton and Charles Schumer, were there, as was Governor George Pataki. The battalion stood at attention in front of a huge audience in the gymnasium as the guests read aloud our accomplishments. The Tenth Mountain Division had been the first to deploy against terrorism. Now we were the first to return and be welcomed home.

That day, we really were made to feel special, if only for a few hours, and I was glad my mother was there to see it. A few of us marched in front of the larger formation and accepted awards for valor in combat. I received my medal from Secretary of the Army Thomas White, and afterward some television crews interviewed my mother and me. She almost choked up in front of a Syracuse newsman when she described my military accomplishments in light of her father's. I don't remember what the secretary said to me. I just remember staring straight ahead and then looking down afterward at the medal and the shiny combat infantrymen's badge he had pinned to my chest.

After we were honored, I fell into the larger formation to pin assorted medals and combat infantrymen badges on my soldiers. I walked down the ranks, while the soldiers handed me their CIBs with the little aluminum backings and let me pin them on. Ray had grabbed a whole handful of the backings—

almost a hundred—and released them onto the floor as a joke just as I stepped in front of him. The soldiers to his right and left suppressed their laughter, and I couldn't help but crack a smile despite the sobriety of the ceremony.

I took special delight in pinning the CIBs on Flash, Wakefield, and Junk as Sergeant Montoya walked with me, helping me along the way. At last I came to Uncle Jesse, whom I made fun of for getting arrested the day before and spending the night in jail. Uncle Jesse told us that he felt his wife had been spending too much time on the computer and that he had responded in a measured way, taking out his frustrations not on his wife but on the computer itself, dragging the monitor outside and beating it with a baseball bat. To this day I have no idea what crime the authorities charged him with. I hadn't been aware assault and battery against a computer monitor was against the New York State penal code.

All the politicians, to their credit, went out of their way to shake our hands in private, away from the media glare, and welcome us home. My mother got Senator Clinton's autograph, and the two of us had our picture taken with Senator Schumer. Governor Pataki surprised me the most when he fought his way through a huge crowd of media to introduce himself and thank me for the job we had done in Afghanistan. I was stunned that the governor would humble himself by going out of his way to speak to me, and I've been a big fan of his ever since. A few weeks later, some of us were invited to the state capital, and Governor Pataki treated us royally.

The next day, my picture was on the front page of the local newspaper, "sharing a laugh" with Hillary Clinton. I sent several copies to my mother because she had left that morning, and a copy of that picture of the senator and me still hangs on the fridge back home in Tennessee. My men teased me mercilessly about being in a picture with the liberal junior senator from New York—and a Clinton no less.

A few days after the ceremony, the company left the post for some much needed rest. The men went back to their hometowns and, in some cases, received hero's welcomes. One soldier, a Navaho Indian from Arizona, returned home to find the entire population of his reservation lining the road to cheer his return. Another soldier worked the morning talk show circuit in Orlando, where morning disk jockeys brought in strippers and exotic dancers in his honor. Captain Rogers went home and cocooned with his wife and new son, leaving us with strict instructions not to call or stop by for at least a week. As usual, I ignored his orders and spoke to him a few times during his leave. He sounded as happy as I have ever heard him, content to spend time behind closed doors, away from the uniform, with his family. He even had me over for dinner one night to show off his son.

I remained on duty at Fort Drum, aware that if I had gone home I too would have been treated like a conquering hero. I had decided that as much as I selfishly desired to be singled out for praise, I paradoxically wanted to be left alone. I had heard that everyone back home had read the *Army Times* article soon after it was published, and this made returning all the more difficult. When my grandfather returned from World War II, he never had to speak about anything that went on in the Pacific while he was fighting the Japanese. For me, though, it was different. Everyone in Chattanooga had a pretty good idea from television and newspaper reports of what I had been through. And because of the *Army Times* article, which my father bought six copies of at the local National Guard armory, everyone back home also knew I had killed someone. So I knew they would not hesitate before asking, "What was it like killing that man?"

The modern media has certainly affected the tact of the public. Because no subject is off-limits on television, people assume no subject is ever off-limits in private. And that's not true. I didn't want to talk about my experiences until I had spent time alone to reflect on them. It had been bad enough when friends started calling me after I returned, wanting to know all about the "kill" they had read about. I had decided not to return to Tennessee until I was ready to answer their questions. It would take several months. I knew which people I wanted to see, and I would in due time. Bobby's wife was still working near the base, so he stayed on as well. But we set lax standards for the guys who remained in the rear detachment, cutting out of work every day at noon and liberally issuing four-day passes over weekends. I used those passes to visit friends in Philadelphia, New York, and Boston on consecutive weekends.

I felt my heart begin to quicken as I drove back into Philadelphia for Penn Relays Weekend. The Penn Relays is the oldest track meet in the United States. As a track enthusiast, I had worked the Relays all four years in college and had met up with my buddy Chaz to watch them the year after graduation, on my way up to Fort Drum after Ranger School. Chaz was one of the most popular students when we were at Penn, a light-skinned black guy from Baltimore with a Barry White voice the women all swooned for. We were polar opposites, of course, and people in school couldn't believe we were such good friends. After all, I was a lanky white kid from East Tennessee with a high-pitched twang and thrice-broken nose who couldn't begin to approach Chaz's handsomeness and cool. For the first few years, we weren't close—we barely knew each other. But when Chaz went through a spiritual transformation and became a Christian at the end of our junior year, we began to share our struggles with faith together and became close.

After graduation, Chaz had headed off to a seminary while I joined the army. We agreed to disagree on the ugly realities of my job. Chaz considered killing to be unconscionable, while I accepted it as a reality of my life. Chaz and I were both Christians, but my faith allowed for armed struggle in the face of evil; in Chaz's view, killing was killing, and prohibited by Exodus 20 regardless of the reasons behind the action. We wrote letters back and forth to each other at a feverish pace after graduation and continued to do so while I was away. I couldn't accept Chaz's pacifism and asked him whether he really thought we would have been better off having never fought the Civil War or World War II. To me, pacifism is a flawed logic, though having seen the horrors and realities of war firsthand, I cannot bring myself to denounce it outright.

On Friday, after the track events had been completed for the evening, Chaz and I grabbed dinner at a Chinese restaurant on Fortieth Street and then headed out for a walk. We walked down Locust Walk and then Walnut Street until we had left University City and stood in Center City on the other side of the Schuylkill River. We proceeded north toward the art museum, walking over the interstate and passing brown-stone houses along Twentieth Street. Along the way, we talked about Chaz's studies in Boston as well as my experiences upon returning to America. I could tell Chaz was holding back, engaging in small talk until he found the right time to ask the other questions I knew he had. He contented himself at first with amusing me with talk about his new ascetic lifestyle. Of course, he was still Chaz and so was hopelessly in love with a girl, his love for whom went unrequited. (Chaz's advances were too much for the poor girl in the end—they would be married scarcely a year later.) In the end, we sat down at a bench near the art museum, and as I looked up I realized that Chaz had been more calculating than I had suspected and had brought me here for a reason.

We sat before the Philadelphia Armenian Sculpture, a representation of the mythic figure Meher with different scenes from Armenian history played out in the fresco on the base of the sculpture. Something about the sculpture moved Chaz—I suppose because of the raw power of the figure chiseled before us or perhaps because it was representative of the Armenians, the first nation to embrace Christianity. Chaz sat for a moment and then asked me about combat and about killing. I could tell he was curious, but not morbidly so like some of my other friends who just wanted to hear about the killing and bloodshed.

Chaz was instead trying to reconnect the two of us after my experiences. Perhaps he wondered if our friendship could ever be the same, or if we were now too different to remain friends. I think he felt lost, unable to understand or even truly conceptualize what I had been through. On the one hand, I think he envied me for my experiences, but also understood that while he had been brought closer to his faith during the past two years, I had been pushed away from mine. I was in a moment in my life in which I was seriously questioning my faith, and it would be almost another year before I could walk into a church again.

I opened up to Chaz that night, but I don't think we ever reached any sort of resolution. Chaz and I stopped writing letters back and forth with the regularity that we once had, and I was left to wonder whether every relationship in my life would be unquestionably altered by my experiences in Afghanistan. Inside, I didn't feel any different. But I wonder how others now see me, those who knew me before and also know what I have done, who I am now.

IN ONE OF the articles that my parents and friends read about me in Afghanistan, the author described me as being twenty-four. I wasn't yet—I was only twenty-three, and my friends kidded me, joking that I had given the reporter false information to make myself sound older. I protested that I had not, I had merely told the reporter that I was about to turn twenty-four—that was the truth—and he had written down my age as twenty-four by mistake. But I notice I chafe now when people remark how young I am to have done the things I did.

What determines age, the years one has lived or the events one has lived through? The best line from my favorite movie as a kid, *Raiders of the Lost Ark,* is delivered when Marion Ravenwood tells a bruised and broken Indiana Jones that he isn't the man she knew ten years ago.

"It's not the years, honey," he quips. "It's the mileage."

On 9/11, I think all of us aged a few years, especially those of us who had come of age during the economic boom of the 1990s. We had been too young to really remember the Cold War, growing up in what we thought to be an American Golden Age and awakened forcefully out of it by four jetliners crashing into America from above.

But just as everyone had aged on that day in September, I had also aged since college, turning myself into a warrior and spilling blood on foreign soil. I had lunch with one of my professors after I returned from Afghanistan and joked with his family about the reporter getting my age wrong.

"I was only twenty-three," I confessed.

"And how old are you now?" the professor's daughter asked.

"Fifty-seven," I deadpanned.

If there is a difference between myself and my friends now, it has more to do with the experiences I have been through. I reject the idea that my persona has somehow unalterably changed during my past few years in the army or as the result of my experiences in Afghanistan. The guy tossing grenades out of the back of the Chinook helicopter in the Shah-e-Kot Valley was the same mischievous kid who used to throw bottle rockets at cars on the highways of Tennessee. I had just done things in Afghanistan that did not reflect any part of my persona that my friends had known. The warrior in me had been there, lying dormant, but had no reason to come to the surface until I was in combat.

In college, one of my fraternity brothers asked me if I thought I could ever kill anyone.

"Sure," I replied.

"But how can you be so sure?" he asked.

I didn't know, but I was sure I could. I didn't have to actually shoot a man to know that the power or inclination to do so was in me all along. So if people think that I have changed into something different than who I was, then they just didn't know me well enough. And if I had lost my innocence somewhere in Afghanistan, well . . . Graham Greene once wrote that "innocence is like a dumb leper who has lost his bell, wandering the world, meaning no harm."

We speak of innocence like it is something to be "lost" only in tragedy, something we should do our best to hold on to no matter what. But what if innocence is something to be shed as we get older and wiser, an outer layer of skin that protects us when we are young but ultimately keeps us from seeing the world as it is?

I no longer wander in the dark as I once did. I feel I know better what the world is really like having seen what I have seen, and I stand now ready to face its realities not out of ignorance but with a calloused knowledge.

I WENT TO VISIT my friend Patch in New York City not long after my return. After the trauma of September 11 and his forced relocation, Patch had moved to Park Slope in Brooklyn, several stops on the subway away from Battery Park City in Manhattan and the ruins of the World Trade Center. But like all my other New York friends who lived through September 11 and its aftermath, Patch had somehow become even more of a New Yorker through his experience. I joked to a friend back home that I was visiting Patch to "remind him he is from Hixson, Tennessee, not the Upper West Side." But as Walker Percy might have written, Patch had become more New York than New Yorkers—"For they didn't know what they were like, and he did." Converts really do make the most fervent believers, and despite or perhaps because of September 11, Patch was committed to New York for the long haul, determined more than ever to make his life in the city.

I showed Patch the pictures I had taken in Kuwait and Afghanistan, pictures of the General Lee and of my platoon after our first combat mission. He in turn showed me the pictures he had taken of that day in September, of the smoke and of the chaos. The day's events deeply traumatized him, as they had every resident of Manhattan, and yet he had the presence of mind to snap away with a disposable camera while the world around him was literally collapsing. He continued to take pictures until the Port Authority police forced him onto a boat headed to New Jersey. The last picture is of him leaving a smoking, broken Manhattan.

XIV

I WOULD LEAVE the Tenth Mountain Division and Fort Drum in November 2002. For the previous six months, since our return from Afghanistan, I had served as the company's executive officer. Captain Rogers was on his way out at the same time I was, en route to a cushy new assignment in Florida, so he was more relaxed during those last few months and let the new first sergeant and me run most of the day-to-day operations of the company. The new first sergeant was a sarcastic but terribly efficient senior noncommissioned officer who had little patience for paperwork or bureaucratic nonsense. We got along great, laughing and joking our way through the daily grind of army life in America.

I had a few good last hurrahs with the boys in those final months. Just before I left my job as platoon leader in May, we had one last live fire exercise together at Fort Drum. We had already begun to change a bit—Sergeant Lane and Sergeant Montoya had moved on to new jobs, new privates had arrived—but the old swagger and proficiency of my now battle-hardened platoon was still there. Ray was in rare form, as were McCauley, Junk, and the rest of the old gang. Flash had moved up in the world, becoming a corporal and team leader, responsible for three junior soldiers. I was initially worried about how he would perform because he had started out so shy around me and the rest of the leaders in the platoon, but he performed at a level nothing less than excellent. It was funny, though, to see him harass, teach, and mentor the new privates as we had done him not seven months earlier.

Once we hit the objective of the live fire exercise, my platoon put on its game face and impressed all who watched. Moving at rapid speed through the buildings of the objective, knocking down targets as fast as they came up, we put on a show for Colonel Matthews. Afterward, he told us that in his twenty-year career spent among three light infantry battalions and two Ranger battalions, we were the most proficient light infantry platoon he had ever seen. It was an enormous compliment, amplified by what he later told the battalion's operations officer with a mixture of awe and admiration: "Exum's platoon looked like fucking Delta Force out there."

When I left the platoon as its leader, Third Platoon was ranked as the best in the battalion. The company was regarded as the best in the brigade.

As the company executive officer, I still got to see everyone on a regular basis. Cooter and Uncle Jesse would come over for training exercises, complaining for my benefit that our company Humvee couldn't hold a candle to the General

Lee. Ray got married in the summer to his Italian fiancée, and Sergeant Rod and I were the groomsmen. Donatella, Ray's wife, always fretted over me, vowing to set me up with one of her friends in Italy. She often had Ray bring food in to fatten me up, and I'd go over to their house for dinner every once in a while. I also often visited Sergeant Montoya and his family. It felt good to be at the Montoya home, teasing his two kids, having his family pray over me before I got back into the car to go home. I felt purified by them after having been so unfulfilled by my vacuous social life as an army bachelor.

That whole summer, I kept promising to go out with the old platoon for a night on the town but never did. The closest I got was the night of Ray's bachelor party, dancing like a fool with the fine women of Watertown in some seedy nightclub. Mostly, though, I kept to myself. I bought a new kayak and spent time whitewater paddling on the Black River as well as cycling through the New York countryside. I competed in a few triathlons that summer and spent time alone unwinding from the past year.

When we went on field exercises, we would walk the eighteen miles or so back from the field to the barracks, and I would walk ahead of the rest of the company, ambushing them along the way with blanks from my weapon to keep them sharp and alert. I always had Flash walk with me to keep me company on the long walk back. By this point, he was a fearsome road marcher, a far cry from the year before when I had to practically carry him to the trucks on that hot day we had spent walking back from our first field problem. He still looked after me, sharing his granola bars and water along the way, asking me how my feet were holding up and running alongside me, matching my every stride, even when I decided to pick up the pace for a mile-long jog after eight miles of walking.

I finally went home for a few weeks that July. My mother's family welcomed me with open arms, keeping things relaxed, knowing that I wanted to avoid a big production and to keep my homecoming at a low key. We had a family-only barbecue on the back porch, and for the only time that year, the whole family—all the cousins and aunts and uncles and my grandmother—was in the same place. My cousins and I quaffed Rolling Rock while I told war stories and played with my mother's dogs. The evening ended with us all having our picture taken, and though I am usually camera shy, I didn't hesitate to throw my arms around my uncle and cousins and mug for the photo. I had missed all of them in the past year and discovered how much I needed them. I needed warm people and smiling faces to come home to. Without them to anchor me, it would have been easy for me to accept a life of nothing but the army and war.

My dad's mother tried to host a homecoming as well, but because I'm really not close with that side of the family, it was forced and awkward. I did get to spend some time with my father, however, and he was genuinely proud, wanting to show me off to his friends and buy me dinner every night. I had always looked up to him when I was little, and now I found he looked up to me. It's a big responsibility being your father's hero, but over the years I had also grown to be his friend. I found he was more open and anxious to talk about his life with me. Perhaps he now felt I had something to say that was worthwhile.

I spent the rest of my leave organizing my meager finances, which had gone ignored for a year, and helping my sister figure out how to pay for her upcoming semester of college. My sister is very different from me, less independent and more social, more emotionally sensitive but less mature than I was at her age. She is also smart, though, enrolled at Vanderbilt University with two majors. In her spare time, she has tutored Jewish kids in Nashville studying for their bar and bat mitzvahs in Hebrew, a language she studied in college. I can only imagine the surprise on the faces of the Jewish parents of Nashville when my sister—a pretty, sweet, and devout Methodist—shows up at their doors to tutor their children in Hebrew. She must be quite the wonder of the Nashville Jewish community.

In October, just before I left, I was still the company's second in command when we left for a rotation to the Joint Readiness Training Center in Louisiana. On the last mission there, we assaulted the urban warfare complex as a brigade, with disastrous results, all chronicled on *USA Today*'s front page as their reporters followed the Tenth Mountain Division in their preparation for the anticipated war in Iraq. Before we had even entered the city, half the company had been "killed" by the opposing force. After Third Platoon's leader was "killed," Captain Rogers ordered me to gather the stragglers and find a way into the city, which I did, leading the men just like in old times. Greg's platoon was mostly intact and still alive, largely due to the efforts of his new platoon sergeant, Ray, who had left our old platoon around the same time I did, to move up in the world.

We fought through the city, losing men along the way and

almost getting "killed" ourselves numerous times. At the end, it was like the last stand of Butch Cassidy and the Sundance Kid. The only soldiers left in the entire company were Captain Rogers, me, and the usual suspects—Junk, McCauley, and maybe four others. Together with Junk and McCauley, I helped to clear three buildings and made it until the last room of the city before we ourselves were "killed." We sat there in satisfied defeat, leaning against a wall, watching the sun rise over the horizon, smoking cigarettes and eating MREs. The "referee" following our little band of survivors angrily realized that the reason we had lived as long as we had was that we had all removed the batteries from our laser sensors, rendering us invulnerable to the opposing force until the referee himself declared us dead. It was a classic example of the old platoon—never playing fair, always doing everything imaginable to win, at all costs. The referee chewed my ass while McCauley, Junk, and the others sat behind me laughing. After actual combat, we had a tough time taking training missions seriously.

In November, I moved south to Savannah, where I took charge of an elite Ranger platoon at a small base there shortly before the war in Iraq. The Rangers were different from my old unit in many ways. All the officers were handpicked, and most of the sergeants had either come up through the ranks in the Ranger battalions or had similarly been hand selected out of "the big army." The soldiers were pretty much the same, though much more physically fit, and motivated to a degree unseen in the Tenth Mountain Division. Everyone in the Rangers had fought to get there, and around 90 percent of my platoon had already graduated from Ranger School, which had been the most difficult ordeal in my life. All I had to distinguish me was my combat record. But my platoon had just returned from a combat tour to Afghanistan of their own, so I wasn't anyone special in that regard either. As for the rest of the battalion, one of the companies held the unique distinction of being the most decorated company in the entire army in the GWOT (Global War On Terror) as the wags in the Rangers called it. On Takur Ghar, several Rangers had earned the Silver Star in the fight for Neil Roberts's body.

Still, leadership is leadership. I soon settled into the new rhythms of my job as a Ranger platoon leader. I did two live fire exercises with my new platoon and discovered they weren't *that* much better than the Gladiators. Of course, they had just returned from combat and were rusty. But nonetheless, I wasn't intimidated.

That Christmas was my first one spent home in two years, and I enjoyed every minute of it. My mother was visibly relieved to have me sitting next to her in church on Christmas eve and by her side as we unwrapped presents on Christmas day. Still, as we made our holiday toasts of scotch, I had trouble forgetting my Christmas eve of a year ago when Ray, Sergeant Rod, and I had gathered around my tiny glass at midnight in Kuwait. In retrospect, I think that Christmas eve will remain in my memories long after the many ones spent at home have faded.

I returned to Savannah just before New Year's. We had plenty of work to do in anticipation of war in Iraq, and I was looking forward to training my men. The Friday after New Year's, though, as I was playing street hockey on a concrete roller rink with all the other officers, one of the other lieutenants tripped and fell onto my foot. I had never been seriously injured in my life. In junior year at Penn, I had crushed two bones in my left hand during a football scrimmage and still managed to play the rest of the season. This time, as the lieutenant rolled onto my foot, I felt my knee snap under me and instantly began screaming in pain.

When the doctors took X-rays, they discovered I had dislocated my knee, torn my anterior cruciate ligament, and broken my tibia lengthwise when the knee popped back into place. I went into surgery later that day as my mother drove down from Chattanooga to be by my side when I awoke. Any chance of me deploying to Iraq with my men was gone, and the doctors told me I would be lucky if I could ever run again. I knew that in all likelihood my military career was over.

I WOULD RECOVER in time, seemingly against all odds, taking every stimulant and dietary supplement known to man in my effort to get back to physical fitness. I went home to Chattanooga while recovering, and after a month, I was swimming between one and three miles a day to keep in shape. I soon returned to Georgia, and after six months, I was jumping out of planes again. In June, my doctors pronounced me eight months ahead of my rehabilitation schedule. After seven months, I was running six-minute miles again.

Still, I missed out on the major combat operations of the war in Iraq, a.k.a. GPWD II (Great Patriotic War in the Desert, Part II). During the first month of the war, my unit helped to rescue Private Jessica Lynch in the first successful rescue operation of an American prisoner of war since the Ranger-led raid on the Cabanatuan prison camp in the Philippines in World War II. I waited by a computer screen during the raid, my crutches by my side, watching the whole rescue go down over the Internet. I have never felt as depressed in my entire life, and all the Rangers stuck in Savannah who knew of the raid got heavily drunk that night on whiskey and beer, with the knowledge they had just missed out on a defining moment in Ranger history.

For my part, I knew I would eventually recover enough to lead a platoon once again. But my surgeons warned me to find another job once my time in the Rangers was done in another year—my knee couldn't take much more running, much less jumping out of planes. If I kept up the pace I was doing, they said, I could expect to have my knee replaced by the age of thirty-five.

I had wisely taken the law school admissions test while home on leave recovering from surgery. Now, more and more, it looked like I would have to trade in my combat fatigues for the civilian dress of a lawyer or journalist.

XV

In the Sunday, December 29, 2002, edition of the *New York Times*, the editors ran a special "Year in Review" calendar. I skipped ahead to March to see what they had to say about Operation Anaconda. I had lived a part of history and was anxious to see what others had to say about what we had done in Central Asia.

But there was no mention of the battles in the *Times* calendar. The death of comedian Milton Berle made the March listing, as did Kmart's announcement that the retailer was closing 284 stores. And, this being the *New York Times*, seven of the March calendar's days were dedicated to the Israeli-Palestinian conflict. I was briefly heartened, though, by the lengthy paragraph titled "A Bloody March" at the very bottom of the month's calendar. After all, it *was* a bloody month. Eight Americans had died in the largest American offensive since the Gulf War. Upward of 450 al-Qaeda and Taliban had also been killed. But, sadly, the paragraph turned out to be another retelling of the violence in the Middle East.

Reading this and all the other end-of-the-year summaries in other periodicals, I became incensed. They hadn't even mentioned—at the very least—any of the American soldiers who had died over there. I was now serving with the Ranger unit that had lost three of its best soldiers in the fight to recover Neil Roberts's body. I was especially upset that the *Times* did choose to run a mention of the errant U.S. bomb that killed forty Afghanis attending a wedding in July, highlighting one of our mistakes but none of the good we did. That particular incident had helped to reignite the philosophical discussion before the Iraq war of whether or not a lost American life somehow counts for more than a lost foreign life. The *New York Times* at least seemed to have set up a neat hierarchy of death and loss. Israeli deaths, apparently, meant more than the deaths of American soldiers. So too did the deaths of Palestinians, Afghanis, B-grade comedians, and everyone else on the food chain.

The following month, as I recovered from my injured leg, I found myself watching a television movie on NBC titled *War Stories*. The plot followed a group of reporters covering a war in a fictional country that looked a lot like Uzbekistan but, yet, was not explicitly Uzbekistan. The lesson I took from the movie was that in the postmodern era, soldiers are not the real heroes of war. They can't be—they're too violent and lack moral purity. In the movie version of events, journalists are the true heroes. They are the ones who risk the most for the most noble cause. And so reporters become the story, with soldiers just window dressing to their journalistic exploits.

With all this on my mind I sat down in a Subway restaurant with Captain Rogers in southeast Georgia in February 2003. My knee was now in a brace, and I propped it up on the bench next to him. We talked about his family, about his new home in Orlando, and about his new assignment. I told him that a publisher had approached me about writing this book, and he surprised me with his enthusiasm for the project. He felt the way I felt, that our story—the story of our men in Afghanistan—needed to be told.

I UNDERSTAND NOW why my grandfather never talked about his service in the Pacific. As a kid, I would find some picture he had taken and ask him to tell me about the war, a deeply romantic thing for me even then. He never would, always sending me on my way disappointed.

After my grandfather died, though, my grandmother gave me the book of pictures he had taken as a young army photographer in Asia. The pictures themselves tell my grandfather's story—his journeys into New Guinea, the Philippines, Okinawa, and Japan. Black-and-white, pasted onto black cardboard paper, the pictures are the only glimpse any of us have ever been given into my grandfather's life during those four years.

In one picture, my grandfather poses with New Guinea natives. The inscription below, written in my grandfather's neat block handwriting, tells the reader this is the first time that any of the New Guineans had seen a white man. There he is, a South Carolina farm boy standing tall among the brown-skinned jungle natives. In another picture, my grandfather is behind a piece of waist-high plywood, bathing himself by his camp in the jungle. His body is tall and muscular but grotesquely thin, much like mine after I graduated from Ranger School. In another picture, a Japanese general lies on a gurney, bleeding from the stomach. The caption below says that he has just attempted hara-kiri.

Most of my grandfather's pictures, the ones from combat, were confiscated by the War Department. But I can imagine what he must have witnessed in the Philippines and on Okinawa. He must have seen enough acts of barbarism and savagery to make his fingers tremble as they adjusted the focus on his lens. He also must have been present at acts of bravery and sacrifice on an epic scale. And that, I think, is why he never spoke about his own experiences. How could he express in words what had occurred, when he had seen the real heroes and had witnessed their deeds? How could he tell stories when all the heroes he knew were killed on those beaches and in those jungles, fighting against the Japanese?

Yet maybe my grandfather's reservations stemmed from something else entirely. Maybe, like my uncle in Vietnam, war stirred something inside him that he was never able to find again as a civilian after the war. Was everything else anticlimactic? Could you ever feel so alive as you did among the dead? Maybe my grandfather had collected and captioned his pictures for me, to tell the story of men braver than he had been. But maybe also he kept his pictures to remember a time during which men were braver, stronger, and far more noble than they would be later in life.

My greatest fear at the age of twenty-five is that my best years are already behind me. I fear that I will never find an opportunity to do so much, to be a part of something so significant as what we did in the aftermath of September 11, when a few thousand American men and even some women traveled halfway across the world to avenge the deaths of their countrymen and set things right in a country we had let foster terrorists who now threatened our freedom.

Reinhold Niebuhr once wrote: "As a collective undertaking war is primarily selfish and immoral without excuse. But for the individual it often means the highest expression of his altruism and the greatest opportunity for the development of his nobler passions." And Walker Percy wrote in the novel *Lancelot*: "The only time members of my family have ever been happy, brave, successful, was in time of war."

I REALIZE THAT to view war in such a romantic light loses sight of its atrocities. Even my brief tour in Afghanistan revealed the legacy of horrors born from two decades of warfare. Men in their twenties had grown up knowing nothing other than war, while warlords roamed the land as the only source of order to be found among the ruins.

That's why the Taliban had been so effective at first. They had stepped into the chaotic void left by the collapse of peace and order that had began with the Soviet invasion of 1979. When no one else could provide law, they did. When no one else could unite the rival tribes, they crushed them and formed a union of their own.

But the fighting didn't stop there. Violence begat violence, and new enemies rose to be fought as soon as the old ones lay dead in the ground.

War will last as long as man remains a sinful creature, flawed as we are and fallen from grace. We should not use that as an excuse to solve all our problems with violence, because peaceful alternatives often exist. But even these must often be backed up by a credible threat of force. Sometimes, war becomes inevitable through the evils of man. Our nation was forced into war on September 11, 2001. When we decide to stop fighting, though, is another matter.

In the end, there is one thing I am sure of. No matter a war's outcome, the soldier never wins.

At the end of a battle, there are no victors among the men who fought the fight. There are the dead, and there are the survivors. And for the survivors the last battle is fought after coming home. After the shooting stops, how does the soldier settle back into society and modern civilization?

I'm still looking for the answer.

But if my grandfather and countless others found it, maybe I can too.

EPILOGUE

I WROTE THIS BOOK at a time in which most of the army was deployed to wars near and far. The platoon I had led a year earlier was now back in Afghanistan after a year at home, trying to preserve the peace for which we had fought.

I think about my men every day, wondering how they are doing, wondering if they are safe, praying they will make it back. Before they left, they would sometimes call me at odd hours in the night, borrowing a prank from Joseph Heller's *Catch-22*, yelling "T. S. Eliot!" into the receiver and hanging up. I always knew by the sound of the voice who had called and would call each back, asking about things at Fort Drum, rumors about the war, and what their plans for the future were.

My men will always be a part of me. They are as much a part of my family as the people in East Tennessee who raised me. In a sense, my men and I came of age together, and for as long as I live they can count on me to be there for them whenever they call. I was their leader once, and now I lead others. But they know they will forever be my responsibility. People sometimes ask me what I am most proud of in my military career, and I tell them that the thing I cherish the most is the trust I was given to lead those men into combat and bring them home. The President and country and army had put their faith in me, but those men trusted me with their lives.

On a cold March morning in 2002, I walked into the Shah-e-Kot Valley. Thirty-three men walked beside me. And no matter where I go, they will always be with me.

AUTHOR'S NOTE

ALL OF THE PEOPLE described in this narrative are real. In several places, I used nicknames or first names in lieu of the real names of soldiers I served with. In some places I have completely changed their names and identities.

ACKNOWLEDGMENTS

I WILL NEVER BE ABLE to pay back the many people who made this book possible. Many thanks go out to Bill Shinker, my publisher, and Daniel Greenberg, my agent. My mentor at the University of Pennsylvania and beyond, Dan Traister, read early drafts of this book and gave invaluable feedback, as did my best friend since the fifth grade, Ben Scott. My mother, the English teacher, corrected most of my grammatical errors, and Neal Pollack, "America's Greatest Living Writer," was my biggest cheerleader from the start. But none of this would have happened if it weren't for my editor, Brendan Cahill, who not only talked me into writing this book but walked with me every step of the way—and graciously put my bar tab on his corporate card at the end of the night. Thanks.